MW00974530

The Gospel Conversationalist

How Jesus Engaged the
Lost in Everyday Life

SAM GREER

WESTBOW
PRESS®
A DIVISION OF THOMAS NELSON
& ZONDERVAN

Copyright © 2018 SAM GREER.

All rights reserved. No part of this book may be used or reproduced by any means, graphic, electronic, or mechanical, including photocopying, recording, taping or by any information storage retrieval system without the written permission of the author except in the case of brief quotations embodied in critical articles and reviews.

Scripture quotations are from the ESV® Bible (The Holy Bible, English Standard Version®), copyright © 2001 by Crossway, a publishing ministry of Good News Publishers. Used by permission. All rights reserved.

WestBow Press books may be ordered through booksellers or by contacting:

WestBow Press
A Division of Thomas Nelson & Zondervan
1663 Liberty Drive
Bloomington, IN 47403
www.westbowpress.com
1 (866) 928-1240

Because of the dynamic nature of the Internet, any web addresses or links contained in this book may have changed since publication and may no longer be valid. The views expressed in this work are solely those of the author and do not necessarily reflect the views of the publisher, and the publisher hereby disclaims any responsibility for them.

Any people depicted in stock imagery provided by Getty Images are models, and such images are being used for illustrative purposes only. Certain stock imagery © Getty Images.

ISBN: 978-1-9736-4304-3 (sc)
ISBN: 978-1-9736-4305-0 (hc)
ISBN: 978-1-9736-4303-6 (e)

Library of Congress Control Number: 2018912361

Print information available on the last page.

WestBow Press rev. date: 10/16/2018

Contents

Foreword

The Gospel is just as powerful and effective today as it was in Paul's day during the launching of the New Testament church. I love hearing stories of pastors, church members and students sharing their stories of engaging people with the Gospel. What an amazing thing to see the simplicity and power of people simply being obedient to tell people about Jesus and giving them an opportunity to respond. Many have seen people respond in faith to Jesus. Others have not responded immediately, but our prayer is that God will place other believers in their path who will also voice their need for the gospel.

I am convinced that the current lack of evangelism we see in many believers and churches is not due to a shortage of evangelism tools. I have used many evangelism tools myself and trained church members to use them. I don't have anything against tools. But as a pastor friend of mine recently told me, "If you know John 3:16 and have a testimony, you can share your faith."

And there is no special power in an evangelism tool. It is simply a way to give believers confidence that they can get out there and talk to people about the gospel.

One of my favorite stories is from my last church, Highview Baptist in Louisville, Ky., when our entire church was doing the FAITH evangelism strategy, the evangelistic tool developed by Bobby Welch while he was pastor at First Baptist Church Daytona Beach, Fla. It became wildly popular among churches in the late 1990's and 2000's and is still used by many today.

One lady in our church refused to learn it. She was petrified of sharing her faith, although you couldn't get her to admit it. Then, when she finally gave in and learned it, she still said she would not share it with anyone. Finally, she decided to go out one night with one of our FAITH outreach groups as they visited with non-attenders in our nearby neighborhoods. Just before the group she was with knocked on the door, this woman announced "Let me do the sharing here."

If you are not familiar with it, the technique helps you walk through the word "Faith" as a way of introducing a person to Jesus. Each letter stands for a point in the presentation. "F" is for forgiveness, which we all need because of sin; "A" is for available, because forgiveness and salvation are available to all of us through Jesus Christ; "I" is for impossible because it is impossible for any of us to get to heaven on our own efforts; "T" is for turn. We must all repent from our sins and turn toward Jesus. "H" is for heaven. If we place our faith in Jesus, he will prepare a place for us in heaven.

So once our group with the reluctant participant introduced themselves and were invited in, it was time to share the reason for their visit. Without much warning, the woman blurted out, "'F' is for forgiveness. Because we are all sinners. 'A' is for available. Salvation is available to everyone."

Then she jumped right over "I," shared "T" and completely forgot "H."

She basically gave the presentation using the word "FAT."

But you know what? The couple she shared with that night said they wanted to repent and ask Jesus to forgive their sins. That woman led this couple to Jesus by sharing "FAT."

I love that example and share it often because it reminds me it's not the tool, it's not about an eloquent presentation. It's not even about getting everything in the right order. It's about being obedient. Caring enough about other people to share with them about the most important thing in your life.

If we speak up—even in the most awkward, stumbling,

bumbling way—the Holy Spirit will do His work in people's hearts and lives. We just need to be obedient.

Recently, my wife Lynette and I had dinner with a young couple from Ghana who had a pretty dramatic story of how they had been falsely arrested and mistreated. We were able to walk them from that experience to a conversation about the gospel and a challenge about their need to respond to Jesus.

Some people ask, "What counts as a gospel conversation?" It needs to be more than just a conversation about God, although sometimes that will be the starting point for some people. A true gospel conversation must have a clear explanation of the gospel and a challenge to the person for their response. We should make it clear to whomever we are talking that it is not just enough to know this information. Jesus challenges us to do something with it. He requires a response.

But at the same time, your conversation should not be one-sided. If you're doing all the talking that's not a conversation—it's a speech. So engage the person just like you would if you were talking about anything else. Ask them questions. Discover where they are coming from on spiritual matters. Do your best to get to know them better through the conversation.

The pages ahead are filled with great reminders for why we do what we do and how we can be more faithful in doing it even better. I am so grateful for Sam and his passion for Jesus. I know that as you are more faithful to share the gospel, God will give you a growing number of people with whom to share it. I hope you will bring others along!

Kevin Ezell
President
North American Mission Board, SBC

Dedication

I dedicate this book to the three ladies in my life: Tonya, Braydee, and Belle.

To my wife, Tonya, your love, support, and partnership in the gospel motivates me every day to live for Jesus. I love you!

Braydee and Belle I thank God that He gave you to your mother and me. Being your dad is teaching me much about God's love. Thank you for reminding me to have gospel conversations!

Introduction

I was born into a fishery family where the motto was "not all fried fish eaters are Greers, but all Greers are fried fish eaters." When pulling up a chair to the table at any Greer family get-together, there was no doubt that fresh fried fish was on the menu. What's more, fresh fried fish was a Greer table staple at Easter, Thanksgiving, Christmas, birthdays, holidays, Mondays, Tuesdays, Wednesdays, Thursdays, Fridays, Saturdays and Sundays! My grandfather, Pawpaw, and his brothers were the patriarchs who not only ate fish but also fished for fish, raised fish, cleaned fish, fried fish, and even served fish at their fish house. The Greers are a family who know how to speak Nemo and Dory's language.

Uncle Anthony tells a story of growing up in such a fish-friendly environment. Being younger and smaller than my dad, Uncle Anthony always looked for an advantage whenever a brotherly fight broke out. Just to the side of their house was a line of cedar trees where Pawpaw used to hang and skin catfish. In that time, if you wanted to learn how to skin a catfish you didn't visit YouTube, you visited PawpawTube on Cedar Tree Lane in Crystal Springs, MS.

On one particular day, when my uncle and dad were engaged in a sibling scuffle, every cedar limb on cedar lane was decorated with a bled-out, ready-to-be-skinned catfish. Quickly getting the upperhand, Uncle Anthony grabbed the tail of one of those catfish with both hands and slugged my dad upside the head. Only in the Greer family would the weapon-of-choice in a sibling rivalry be a catfish!

For me, growing up in the Greer family left little room for not enjoying eating fish. The only thing worse than growing up in the Greer family and not enjoying eating fish was growing up in the Greer family and being allergic to fish and unable to eat it. Yes, I was allergic to fish. Yes, I am still allergic to fish and unable to eat it.

Although allergic to fish, fishing with fishermen for fish was still a significant part of my childhood. We spent our summer mornings and nights jug fishing, crappy fishing, and bass fishing. Whether we were fishing from the bank or from a boat, we were fishing for the purpose of catching fish. Although still allergic to fish, to this day, fishing is my favorite outdoor activity; more specifically, bass fishing was my favorite outdoor activity.

Fishing with Jesus' fishermen for men is a significant part of my life today. Although Jesus has called His followers to be "fishers of men," too many believers behave as if they are allergic to "fishing for men" (personal evangelism).

Have you ever frozen in fear when you have thought about talking to someone about the good news of Jesus? Have you ever dodged sharing your faith in Christ as if it was a deadly substance to which your spiritual immune system is allergic? Have you ever avoided, like the plague, an opportunity to tell somebody about Jesus? Are you terrified to talk to another person about the gospel? Are you allergic to opening your mouth and telling people the good news? Do you feel ill equipped to share your faith in Christ? Could it be that you feel as if your spiritual IQ is insufficient to share the gospel? Is it possible that you believe you need to learn more before you share anymore? If so, you are not alone!

According to *Christianity Today's* Chris Lutes, *'I'm not smart enough'* is the top reason of seven reasons given for not sharing Christ. He wrote, "Jesus' disciples weren't known for their brains or their theology degrees. They were pretty ordinary guys, really."[1] Lutes points to the Apostle Luke's writing in Acts 4:13 as an example:

Now when they saw the boldness of Peter and John, and perceived that they were uneducated, common men, they were astonished. And they recognized that they had been with Jesus."[2]

Knowing more about Jesus is no match for *knowing Jesus more.* Lutes concluded with some encouraging words for believers, "You are smart enough to tell others about Jesus because you have a friendship with Him. And the closer you get to Him, and the better you know Him, the more you'll have to say about Him."[3]

The purpose of this book is to encourage and equip every follower of Christ to be a gospel conversationalist. Do you consider yourself a conversationalist? Does engaging in conversation come easy for you? Or, do you often *feel "not smart enough"* to engage in a conversation about Jesus? Whether being conversational comes easy for your or not, any and every follower of Jesus can become a gospel conversationalist. Being a gospel conversationalist is more about *who you know* than it is about *what you know* or *how much you know.*

By considering Jesus' conversational approach to sharing the truth of the gospel, this book seeks to mine through some of Jesus' encounters and one-on-one conversations for applicable principles for becoming a gospel conversationalist. A gospel conversationalist is one who, like Jesus, engages the lost in everyday life. Jesus can help you overcome your personal evangelism allergies! Are you ready to become a gospel conversationalist?

Jesus Is the Original Gospel Conversationalist

"Since we have a great high priest who has passed through the heavens, Jesus, the Son of God, let us hold fast our confession. For we do not have a high priest who **is unable to sympathize with our weaknesses**, but one who in every respect has been tempted as we are, yet without sin. Let us then with confidence draw near to the throne of grace, that we may receive mercy and find grace to help in time of need."

Hebrews 4:14-16

What the Gospel Says

What is the gospel? The word *gospel,* in the Greek, simply means *good news.* The gospel, then, is God's eternal good news of hope found only in the death, burial, and resurrection of Jesus. In 1 Corinthians 15:3, Paul the apostle defined the gospel as "Christ died for our sins in accordance with the Scriptures, that he was buried, that he was raised on the third day in accordance with the Scriptures."

The gospel is neither reformed nor non-reformed theology, it is not doctrine, it is not social justice, it is not politics, it is not patriotism, it is not religion, nor is it tradition. The gospel never has to adapt to the culture, either by having something added to it or by being softened to become relevant.

What the gospel says is simple yet profound. The gospel says Jesus lived a life we couldn't live, died a death we should've died, and rose from the dead proving He alone can forgive sin. The gospel says God has done for us, in and through the life, death, burial and resurrection of Jesus, what we could never do for ourselves.

In 2 John 3, the disciple whom Jesus loved offers a helpful summary of what the gospel *says*:

> Grace, mercy and peace will be with us, from God
> the Father and from Jesus Christ the Father's Son,
> in truth and love.

In this verse, there are at least 5 statements made by the gospel of Jesus.

1. The gospel says, "We are saved *by* something." The first word in 2 John 3, *grace*, describes the glorious truth that we are saved *by* something. The word *grace* is defined and must be understood as "unearned good will, unmerited favor and an undeserved gift of kindness." Grace can be characterized as we *get* what we don't *deserve*.

Grace says we can't save ourselves with our goodness. No amount of good abilities, good attitudes, good behavior, good conduct, good deeds, good education, good effort, good habits, good intentions, good morals, good progress, good reputation, good success, good tradition, or good works has any hope of saving us. We are saved *by* grace alone.

Grace says we can't save ourselves with our sacrifices. No amount of sacrificial talents, sacrificial time or sacrificial treasures has any hope of saving us. In June of 2006, Warren Buffet, the world's second-richest man at the time, announced that he would donate 85% of his $44 billion fortune to five charitable foundations.

Commenting on this extreme level of generosity, Buffet said: "There is more than one way to get to heaven, but this is a great way."[4] Untrue: we are saved *by* grace alone.

Grace says we can't save ourselves with our religion. No amount of church attendance, religious study, religious rituals, number of baptisms or Lord Supper observances has any hope of saving us. Dr. Chuck Herring, while leading First Baptist Collierville in the observance of the Lord's Supper, said: "This table of the Lord isn't where sinners find Christ, but where sinners celebrate being found by Christ."[5] We are saved *by* grace alone.

Oh, how we are so prone to take credit for the fact that we are saved, being saved, and will be saved. I was reminded of this on a Friday in late June when my family headed off for a day at Dollywood in Pigeon Forge, TN. A few days before we went to Dollywood, my wife Tonya let our nine-year-old daughter Belle try using her Fitbit. Belle was so excited to see how many steps she could get on the Fitbit for the week. When she found out we were going to Dollywood, she couldn't wait to see how many steps she would step.

We arrived at Dollywood about 10:30 a.m. and parked in parking lot C, as parking lot A and B were full. The line to ride the trolley from the parking lot to the park entrance was terribly long. So, we decided to walk from parking lot C to the park entrance. You would have thought that we had been in the park all day long and were completely worn-out, as Belle was devastated that we had to walk so far. She said, "My legs are killing me. I am so tired." I said, "We have been riding in a car for two hours and thirty minutes. Besides, the reason you are wearing the Fitbit is to see how many steps you can step."

Belle was moving like a cramping runner at the end of a marathon. She looked as exhausted as a World Cup soccer player after playing through two halves, through stoppage time, through extra time, and through penalty kick time. Until, that is, we arrived at the park entrance. Then, suddenly, a miracle happened. Her legs came to life; they were as fresh as a World Cup substitution player entering late into the game. Belle started running toward the Thunderhead rollercoaster. She sprinted to the Wild Eagle. She cross-country ran to the Tennessee Tornado. Belle ran all over Dollywood that day.

Belle outran Forrest Gump until, that is, we arrived at the park exit at the end of the day. Then, suddenly, her legs no longer worked. The line to take the trolley back to the parking lots was as long as the line at the start of the day. So, once again, we decided to walk to parking lot C, except for Belle. She was too tired to walk. In the 90-degree plus heat, I put Belle on my shoulders and began the arduous trek to parking lot C.

By the time we reached parking lot A, sweat was running down my face as I looked over at the trolley dropping folks off. I made eye contact with a family on the trolley. We looked at one another with a look of inferiority and a smirk of judgment. I imagined them thinking: "Why are you walking when you *could* be riding this trolley?" I thought: "Why are you riding the trolley when you *should* be walking?" Meanwhile, Belle had a bag of cotton candy in her hand that was sticking to my face. The sweat from my forehead, mixed with the sugar from Belle's cotton candy, was burning my pupil, turning my retina red and covering my cornea.

At this juncture, I was struggling. We finally got to parking lot B, one lot closer to parking lot C, and it happened. As I was walking, I felt something vibrate. I realized it was the Fitbit on Belle's arm that was vibrating on my arm. The Fitbit was registering the steps I was taking although it was on Belle's arm and not mine. Right after the vibration, Belle said exuberantly: *"Daddy, I just made my steps!"*

Before I said what I wanted to say, the Holy Spirit pierced my heart. You know those fleeting, teachable moments in life when the Holy Spirit impresses a lesson on your heart. Yes, this was one of those moments.

As Belle's father, I was the one physically carrying her in that moment; however, Belle was more than willing to take credit for making *her* steps. The Holy Spirit placed this question on my heart and mind: *"How many times have you taken credit for the grace given you by your Heavenly Father?"* How many times have you said: *"Father, I just won those people to Christ! Father, I just preached the best sermon ever! Father, I just gave the best gift ever! Father, I just made the greatest sacrifice ever! Father, I just _____!"*

God saves us *by* His grace. God keeps us *by* His grace. God carries us *by* His grace. We are saved, kept, and carried *by* grace alone! The gospel says we are saved *by* something!

2. The gospel says, "We are saved *from* something." The second word in 2 John 3, *mercy*, emphasizes the fact that we are saved *from* something. The word *mercy* carries the idea of "compassion, kindness or concern expressed for someone in need." Mercy is defined as God not *giving* what we *deserve*. While grace says "We are saved *by* something," *mercy* says "We are saved *from* something." What is it exactly that we are saved from?

Paul the apostle, in Ephesians 2:1-5, identified what a sinner needs to be saved from:

> And you were dead in the trespasses and sins in which you once walked, following the course of this world, following the prince of the power of the air, the spirit that is now at work in the sons of disobedience—among whom we all once lived in the passions of our flesh, carrying out the desires of the body and the mind, and were by nature, children of wrath, like the rest of mankind. But God, being rich in mercy, because of the great love with which he loved us, even when we were dead in our trespasses, made us alive together with Christ.

We are saved from death. Outside of a relationship with Christ, sinners are dead spiritually. Why? A person must be born again to avoid spiritual death. Each sinner can either be born once (physically) and die twice (physically and spiritually), or be born twice (physically and spiritually) and die once (physically).

According to Revelation 1:5, Jesus is the "firstborn of the dead." What does that mean? Jesus wasn't the first to live, to die or even to be raised from the dead. But Jesus is the first to live, to die and to be raised to life to never die again. Jesus alone saves us from death! We are saved from our sin. All men, women, boys and girls are sinners, and all sinners sin by nature and by choice. The penalty of sin is death and the power of sin keeps us from being free, while the presence of sin will never be escaped this side of heaven. Salvation means that we are immediately saved from the penalty of sin; we are being saved from the power of sin, and we will be saved from the presence of sin in heaven. Jesus alone saves us from sin!

We are saved from God's wrath. Outside of a relationship with Jesus, we remain under the wrath of God. God's wrath was satisfied in Jesus' sacrifice on the cross. If a person rejects Jesus and His sacrifice on the cross, then that person must satisfy God's wrath by being separated from God forever on the Day of Judgment. By nature we are all children of wrath. But by the mercy of God we don't have to remain children of wrath; rather, by putting our faith in Jesus, we become children of God. Jesus alone saves us from God's wrath!

We are saved from the Devil's hell. Hell may not be popular, but hell is biblical. Hell is a real place. Hell is a really hot place. Hell is a real place of torment, punishment, regret, separation and suffering. People in hell will never be annihilated. People in hell will always suffer unspeakable wrath.

Hell is a place you don't want to go. Hell is a place you don't have to go. In Matthew 25:41, Jesus identified hell as a place of "eternal fire prepared for the devil and his angels." Don't dismiss hell, miss hell! In his sermon "Presumptuous Sins," C. H. Spurgeon quoted Jonathan Edwards:

> Sinner, remember thou art at this moment standing over the mouth of hell upon a single plank and that plank is rotten. Thou art hanging over the jaws

of perdition by a solitary rope and the strands are creaking—breaking now, and yet thou talkest of tomorrows.[6]

Jesus alone saves us from the Devil's hell.

The Bible says, in Lamentations 3:23, that God's mercies are "new every morning." I am so grateful that God's mercies are *new* every morning because God's mercies are what I *need* every morning. Post Lamentations 3:23 on your bathroom mirror so that you will be reminded everyday that the gospel says we are saved *from* something.

3. The gospel says "We are saved *to* something." In 2 John 3, the word *peace* reminds us that we are saved *to* something. We are saved to be at peace with God and to have the peace of God. Peace is never the absence of affliction, hardship, conflict, suffering, or trouble. Peace is the presence of Jesus in the midst of all life's troubles. One will never experience peace without first encountering grace. Peace is the application of God's grace and mercy in our hearts and lives.

John makes it crystal clear in 2 John 3 that peace "will be with us." In the Greek, the end of 2 John 2 reads "with us will be forever" while the beginning of 2 John 3 reads "will be with us grace, mercy and peace." Put those together and the original language reads "with us will be forever, will be with us grace, mercy and peace." John is not offering some wishful-thinking, pie-in-the-sky, hope-so salvation; he is offering a know-so salvation.

We are saved to an assurance of salvation. In Christ, we are not walking around hoping without any hope. The gospel of Jesus assures us that we are saved, being saved, and will be saved. John walked with Jesus. John talked with Jesus. John touched Jesus. John saw Jesus. John has no doubt that "grace, mercy, and peace will be with us."

We are saved to the Body of Christ. By the use of the personal pronoun "us" in 2 John 3, John includes himself in those who have grace, mercy, and peace. John is not pointing the finger saying,

"Y'all really need some grace, but I don't." No, John recognized that all who are saved by the grace of God are saved to the Body of Christ. When you belong to Christ, you belong to Christ's Body, the universal church.

We are saved to be a part of a local church. Too many people live their lives with the attitude, "I love Jesus, but I can't stand the church." To say that is to say "I love Jesus, but I don't love what Jesus loves." Others say, "I don't have to be a part of a local church to be a follower of Jesus."

Research from the Pew Research Center suggests that "Young people like the Bible but not church."[7] True, church attendance saves no one; however, to be a follower of Jesus and not be connected to a local church would be a foreign concept to any follower of Jesus in the first century. Are there any specific Scriptures that speak to the necessity of local church membership? Most of the New Testament, from the book of Acts to Revelation, was written to and for the local church. The gospel says we are saved *to* something!

4. The gospel says, "We are saved *through* something." In 1 and 2 John, John was dealing with false teachers who denied that Jesus was the Christ, the Father's Son. In 2 John 3, the apostle whom Jesus loved shared the source of salvation as being "from God the Father and from Jesus Christ the Father's Son." John's emphasis on Jesus being the Father's Son reminds us that we are saved by grace alone, *through* faith alone, in Christ alone.

In Philippians 3:8-9, Paul echoed John's soteriology when he stated:

> For his sake I have suffered the loss of all things and count them as rubbish, in order that I may gain Christ and be found in him, not having a righteousness of my own that comes from the law, but that which comes *through faith in Christ,* the righteousness from God that depends on *faith.*

In Ephesians 2:8, Paul also explained that we are saved by grace "through faith."

We are saved *through* faith, not by sight. Sight equals seeing what is seen. Faith equals seeing what is unseen. We are not saved through what is seen, we are saved through what is unseen. We are saved the same way Abraham was saved. Dr. Tommy Vinson explained it this way:

> Abraham was saved through faith by looking forward to the promised Messiah. Abraham's salvation through faith worked similar to the faith required to use a credit card. When making a purchase on a credit card one understands that a payment will be made sometime in the future. As Abraham believed God, he had faith that Messiah was coming sometime in the future. Our salvation through faith works similar to the faith required to use a gift card. When making a purchase with a gift card one understands that a payment has already been made. As we believe God, we have faith that Jesus, the Messiah, has already come and paid our penalty in full by dying on the cross, being buried, and being raised to life.[8]

The world says "believe in the seen" while the Word says "believe in the unseen."

In a March 2018 article, Esquire Magazine reported that as more and more people become alienated from religion, Google is becoming a god. The author argued:

> Think back on every fear, every hope, every desire you've confessed to Google's search box and then ask yourself: Is there any entity you've trusted more with your secrets? Does anybody know you better

than Google? Google is the closest thing to an omniscient entity. Google is omnipre-sent. Google answers prayers (do a search for all your questions and problems). Google is potentially immortal. Google is infinite. Google remembers all. Google can "do no evil" (omnibenevolent). According to Google trends, the term "Google" is searched for more than "God or Jesus." Is Google our modern-day god?[9]

We are saved *through* faith in God, not *through* faith in Google. We are saved not *through* faith in a Google search; we are saved *through* faith in the Head of God's Church. The gospel says we are saved *through* faith in Jesus Christ.

5. The gospel says, "We are saved *for* something more." 2 John 3 concludes with the phrase "in truth and love." John uses the word *truth* to refer to the embodiment of the gospel. Jesus, the Incarnate God, came into this world full of truth because Jesus is the personification of truth. In John 1:14, the Bible says:

> And the Word became flesh and dwelt among us,
> and we have seen his glory, glory as of the only Son
> from the Father, full of grace and truth.

John uses the word *love* to refer to the unconditional *agape* love that God has for us. *Agape* love has been defined as an "unconditional commitment to an imperfect person."[10] The fact that we are saved *for* something more is underscored by John's use of the phrase "truth and love."

The world says "truth OR love" while the Word says "truth AND love." The world's #LoveWins erroneously argues that truth is relative at best and irrelevant at worst. The world says that love is about feelings and feelings are more important than facts. The world says when feelings are involved, facts don't matter. The world says love without truth conquers all. The world is wrong!

The truth is that *love without truth* OR *truth without love* are both deadly dangerous. Truth without love leads to legalism and pushes people away from the gospel. Love without truth is based on feelings and never leads to the gospel. The Word says we are to "love in truth" and we are to "speak the truth in love." The Word says "truth" AND "love." The Word says "both/and" not "either/ or." The Word is right!

We are saved *for* something more. We are saved to go deeper in the truth. In John 17:17, Jesus prayed to the Father "Sanctify them in the truth; your word is truth." For us to go deeper in the truth, we must go deeper in the Word of God. We must read the Word, so the Word can read us. We must study the Word, so the Word can study us. We must live in the Word, so the Word can live in us. As a pastor friend of mine has said, "We don't need anymore Bible studies, we need to study the Bible more."

At the 2018 Southern Baptist Convention, the SBC Discipleship Task Force reported out their findings of a one-year study on the state of discipleship in Southern Baptist churches. The task force discovered that although SBC churches baptized 7.1 million people over the past twenty years, attendance in those same churches declined in that same time period. The Discipleship Task Force's recommendation to right the ship of discipleship is below:

> Churches need to increase efforts toward Bible engagement. Bible engagement is more than just reading the Word, it is allowing the Word of God & God himself to lead us, and change our direction, our actions and our thinking.[11]

We can engage the Bible more by journaling through the Word, memorizing the Word, praying through the Word, obeying the Word, and being accountable to others as we read the Word.

Journaling through the Bible is an effective way to go deeper in the Word. What is required to journal through the Bible? How do we start? Where do we start? Journaling through the Bible requires three essentials: (1) Textbook, (2) Tool and (3) Time.

- First, our textbook is the Word of God.
- Second, "Journal through the WORD" is an effective tool that can help you go deeper in the Word. **See Appendix A.**
- Third, we are all given 604,800 seconds each week. Journaling twenty minutes a day five days a week equals 6,000 seconds per week. 6,000 seconds is less than 1% of your allotted 604,800 seconds each week. Would you be willing to invest less than 1% of your time to see 100% of your life impacted?

We are saved *for* something more. We are saved to love others by engaging in gospel conversations. We are saved to share the truth in love. Followers of Jesus are *never* responsible for saving, but we are *always* responsible for sharing. No one can save anyone, but everyone can share with someone. The gospel says we are to share the truth of the gospel in love, and a key way to do that is through gospel conversations.

Chuck Lawless offered 9 reasons Christians don't share their faith in Christ. He described the sixth reason as follows:

> We've "gotten over" our salvation. When Jesus becomes routine to us—that is, our passion for Him has settled into mediocrity—we won't readily tell others about Him.[12]

How could we ever get over the gospel, which says we are saved *by* something, *from* something, *to* something, *through* something and *for* something more?

What a Gospel Conversationalist Says

As stated in the introduction, being a gospel conversationalist is more about *who you know* than *what you know.* Sure, being biblical is an essential aspect of becoming a gospel conversationalist. Being intentional, respectful, understandable, practical and conversational are also vitally important to becoming a gospel conversationalist. What exactly is a gospel conversationalist? Let's first define the term *conversationalist.*

According to Merriam-Webster a conversationalist is "one who converses a great deal or who excels in conversation."[13] Similarly, the Cambridge Dictionary defines conversationalist as "someone who enjoys or is good at talking with people."[14]

Webster's II New College Dictionary chimes in with its own definition as "one skilled at or given to conversations."[15] Finally, the English Oxford Dictionary defines a conversationalist as "a person who is good at or fond of engaging in conversation."[16]

Based on the definitions above, you may not identify yourself as a conversationalist. Whether you identify as a conversationalist or not, any follower of Jesus can become a gospel conversationalist. How is that possible?

When conversing about the gospel, a person never has to be a political filibuster trying to come up with more to say. A gospel conversationalist is one who *has something to say* (the gospel), rather than one who *has to say something.* A gospel conversationalist is one who is fond of engaging in a conversation about the good news of Jesus. The more you get to know Jesus the more you will want to tell others about Him.

What is it that a gospel conversationalist says? First, a gospel conversationalist presents the gospel. A clear, concise presentation of the death, burial and resurrection of Jesus is essential for any and every gospel conversation.

In 2 Timothy 4:5, toward the end of his life, Paul the apostle reminded Timothy to "do the work of an evangelist and fulfill your ministry." In his last letter, Paul could have explained to Timothy the relationship between God's sovereignty and the free will of man. He could have argued for either God's choosing of man or man's choosing of God. Paul could have listed reasons why he was reformed or non-reformed. Yet, the Holy Spirit's message through Paul was clear "do the work of an evangelist."

As followers of Jesus, we are not called to do the work of a *Calvinist*, nor the work of an *Arminianist*, rather we are called to do the work of an *evangelist*. We are called to be gospel *conversationalists*. Let's stop arguing with one another about the gospel, and let's start agreeing to share the gospel with others. A gospel conversationalist gives a clear presentation of the gospel.

A gospel conversationalist says what the gospel says. After giving a clear gospel presentation, a gospel conversationalist will offer a simple gospel invitation. Some transitional questions are helpful to guide a gospel presentation into a gospel invitation. For example:

- *What questions do you have about what I have shared with you?*
- *Is there anything about the good news of Jesus that you don't understand?*
- *What is keeping you from making a decision to put your faith in Jesus?*
- *Would you like to trust in Jesus right now?*

In his book, *Share Jesus Like it Matters*, Steve Gaines provides this helpful transitional question: "If this [gospel presentation] makes sense to you, is there any good reason why you should not receive Jesus as your Savior and Lord right now?"[17]

Engaging in conversation can be intimidating. Engaging in a gospel conversation can be outright terrifying. Speaking in front of people, whether it was a small group or a large group, was one of my greatest fears growing up. Because of that fear, the last junior college class I enrolled in was Public Speaking. One of the class requirements was to write and deliver a speech. The life and career of Morton Anderson, long-time kicker of the New Orleans Saints, was the subject of my speech. Although terribly nervous, I enjoyed speaking about my favorite football team's Hall of Fame kicker.

People are passionate about certain topics. My wife, Tonya, is passionate about essential oils. Because she has spent time learning about the different oils and experiencing their applications, Tonya loves to talk to anyone, anywhere, anytime about the benefits of essential oils. After giving a presentation about essential oils, she then offers an invitation to use essential oils. A gospel conversationalist is passionate about giving a gospel presentation and extending a gospel invitation.

Being aware of *what* a gospel conversationalist says is important, but learning *how* to say it is critical. The next section focuses on *how* the original gospel conversationalist said *what* He said.

What the Original Gospel Conversationalist Said

Jesus is the original gospel conversationalist. Hebrews 4:14-16 gives us reason enough to know that Jesus is the original gospel conversationalist. In Hebrews 4:14-16, the Bible says:

> Since then we have a great high priest who has passed through the heavens, Jesus, the Son of God, let us hold fast our confession. For we do not have a high priest who is unable to sympathize with our weaknesses, but one who in every respect has been tempted as we are, yet without sin. Let us then with confidence draw near to the throne of grace, that we may receive mercy and find grace to help in time of need.

Jesus' passing "through the heavens" is in reference to His ascension back to the right hand of the Father. Jesus was born in the flesh, lived a sinless life, died a sinner's death on the cross, was buried, and rose from the grave. After appearing to 500+ witnesses in His resurrected body, Jesus "passed through the heavens" back to the Father's side.

In Hebrews 4:15, the Bible says that Jesus is able to "sympathize with our weaknesses." Jesus came to this earth not to exploit us, but to sympathize with us. He came to relate to us, not to retaliate against us. In Luke 19:10, Jesus said "...the Son of Man came to seek and to save the lost." Jesus came to save us by telling us *who He is,* not to impress us by telling us *what all He knows.*

Jesus' IQ -- intelligence quotient -- is second to none. Although Jesus didn't come to tell us *what all He knows,* His intelligence was second to none. The Pharisees, the Scribes, and others often tried to outsmart Jesus but failed every time. Why did they fail? Jesus is the Creator of all things, including IQs. Jesus not only has the highest IQ of any person who has ever walked planet earth, He created intelligence. The Scripture tells us that Jesus knows the heart of man. He knows where people are, who people are, and what people have done.

The only place in Scripture where the Bible indicates that Jesus doesn't know something is in reference to His Second Coming. In Matthew 24:36, Jesus said, "But concerning that day and hour no one knows, not even the angels of heaven, nor the Son, but the Father only." Obviously, Jesus was more interested in telling people to be ready for His coming and less interested in emphasizing a Divinely-intelligent end-times date prediction!

Our world holds those with high IQ's in high regard. In fact, students with the highest GPA's, highest ACT's and highest SAT's receive the most coveted scholarships. Stanford University ranks as one of the toughest schools to grant admission. The average GPA for accepted Stanford students is 4.18 (out of 4.0).[18]

Though held in the highest regard, people with higher intelligence are often outperformed by people with average intelligence. Travis Bradberry and Jean Greaves noted:

People with the highest levels of intelligence (IQ) outperform those with average IQs just 20 percent of the time, while people with average IQs outperform those with high IQs 70 percent of the time. This anomaly threw a massive wrench into what many people had always assumed was the source of success—IQ. Scientists realized there must be another variable that explained success above and beyond one's IQ, and years of research and countless studies pointed to emotional intelligence (EQ) as the critical factor.[19]

Jesus' EQ – emotional quotient -- is second to none. Jesus came to this earth with all the emotions available to Him that we have available to us. Unlike us, Jesus implemented emotional intelligence with perfection. What is emotional intelligence?

Daniel Goleman defined emotional intelligence as "the capacity for recognizing our own feelings and those of others, for motivating ourselves, and for managing our emotions well in ourselves and in our relationships."[20] According to Roy Oswald and Arland Jacobson, "Emotional intelligence has to do with how we manage our emotions so as to function effectively in relationships."[21]

In a Harvard Business Review article, Goleman offered five components of emotional intelligence: (1) self-awareness, (2) self-regulation, (3) motivation, (4) empathy and (5) social skills.

- **Self-awareness** speaks to the ability to recognize and understand your emotions.
- **Self-regulation** speaks to the ability to be able to think before acting.
- **Motivation** is a passion to work for reasons that go beyond money or status.

- **Empathy** is the ability to understand the emotional state and make up of other people.
- **Social skills** speaks of the proficiency in managing relationships and building networks.[22]

Jesus not only mastered these five components of EQ, He is the Master of everything. As the Master, Jesus knew how to masterfully balance His IQ and EQ to *speak the language* of each person He ever encountered. He knew the best way to emotionally, intellectually, and spiritually connect with people to *speak their language*. Jesus spoke to the fishermen differently than He spoke to the Samaritan woman, which was different than how He spoke to Nicodemus.

As 100% God, Jesus' IQ (intelligence) is second to none. As 100% man, Jesus' EQ (emotional intelligence) was also second to none. Although Jesus knows all our dirt, He doesn't turn us back to dirt. He empathizes with us at our dirtiest. Jesus didn't come to this earth *emphasizing His IQ*. He came *emphasizing His EQ*.

Jesus came to this earth to *speak the language* of all men, women, boys and girls and to train His disciples to do the same. He didn't come to this earth to only *speak the language* of Mensa. Mensa is an organization whose members have an IQ of 140 or higher. At a Mensa convention in San Francisco the following happened:

> Several Mensa members lunched at a local San Francisco café. While dining, they discovered that their saltshaker contained pepper and their peppershaker was full of salt. How could they swap the contents of the bottles without spilling, and using only the implements at hand? Clearly this was a job for Mensa! The group debated and presented ideas, and finally came up with a brilliant solution involving a napkin, a straw, and an empty saucer. They called the waitress over to dazzle her with their solution. "Ma'am," they said, "we couldn't help

but notice that the peppershaker contains salt and the saltshaker..." "Oh," the waitress interrupted. "Sorry about that." She unscrewed the caps of both bottles and switched them.[23]

May we be less like the members of Mensa, who were egocentric as they emphasized their IQ, and may we be more like the waitress, who was sympathetic as she emphasized her EQ. In Matthew 5:13 and 14, Jesus told His followers, "You are the salt of the earth.... You are the light of the world." Isn't it time followers of Jesus were sympathetic to the earth and the world by passing the salt and turning on the light?

As gospel conversationalists we should follow after the original gospel conversationalist by being more interested in sharing *who we know* and less interested in sharing *what all we know*. According to the four Gospels, Jesus spent 73% of his time with the few and 27% of his time with the crowds. He was involved in forty-three events with the twelve disciples and seventeen events with the masses.[24] In the remaining chapters, this book presents some of Jesus' encounters and one-on-one conversations to see *how* Jesus *spoke the language* of those He engaged.

Jesus Spoke the Fishermen's Language

"While walking by the Sea of Galilee, he saw two brothers, Simon (who is called Peter) and Andrew his brother, **casting a net into the sea**, for they were fishermen. And he said to them, 'Follow me, and I will **make you fishers of men.**' Immediately they left their nets and followed him. And going on from there he saw two brothers, James the son of Zebedee and John his brother, in the boat with Zebedee their father, **mending their nets**, and he called them. Immediately they left the boat and their father and followed him"

Matthew 4:18-20

"Now the eleven disciples went to Galilee, to the mountain to which Jesus had directed them. And when they saw him, they worshiped him, but some doubted. And Jesus came and said to them, 'All authority in heaven and on earth has been given to me. Go therefore and **make disciples** of all nations, baptizing them in the name of the Father and of the Son and of the Holy Spirit, teaching them to observe all that I have commanded you. And behold, I am with you always to the end of the age.'"

Matthew 28:16-20

Jesus Spoke to the Fishermen

Before touring the Holy Land, I never liked hearing "Visiting the Holy Land makes the Bible come to life." In Hebrews 4:12, the Bible says the Bible is "living and active." Whether one visits the Holy Land or not, the Bible is already alive! After traveling to Jerusalem, I still cringe when I hear people say that taking a trip to the Holy Land "makes the Bible come to life." Yet, I concur that prior to visiting the Holy Land, engaging the Bible is like watching TV in *black and white*, but after a trip to Jerusalem, engaging the Bible is like watching *High Definition* TV.

A Holy Land Tour is pregnant with many Spirit-filled experiences. One such personal experience further cemented my desire to share the good news of Jesus' resurrection. In Jerusalem, one of the holiest sites for Jews is a building on Mount Zion known as the Tomb of David. Some consider the entombed Tomb of David in the City of David as the place where the buried bones of King David still lie. Others offer alternative burial sites for the bones of David. Whether they're on Mount Zion or somewhere else, all Jews recognize that David's bones are still buried somewhere.

Jerusalem has a place where some believe David's bones are still buried; however, Jerusalem has no place where anyone believes that Jesus' bones are still buried. Sure, there is an empty tomb where Jesus was buried, but no entombed tomb where Jesus is still buried. David died and was buried. Jesus died and was buried, but He was raised bodily from the grave. Jesus walked out of the grave, so we could walk in His grace! Jesus exited the grave, so we could enter His grace! Jesus is alive!

Of all the experiences of an eleven-day trip to the Holy Land, visiting the Galilee was the most memorable. I will never forget floating in a boat in the middle of the Sea of Galilee while listening to our pastor present a devotional about Jesus calming the storm on that very sea. To spend time at that place, where Jesus spent time with those He spent most of His time with, was indescribable.

On one such occasion, Matthew recorded the incident when Jesus called His disciples to follow Him. In Matthew 4:18, the former tax collector wrote, "While walking by the Sea of Galilee, he saw two brothers, Simon (who is called Peter) and Andrew his brother." Before Jesus *spoke the language of the fishermen*, Jesus *spoke to the fishermen*. Prior to *speaking to the* fishermen, Jesus *saw the fishermen*.

While walking by the Sea of Galilee, Jesus could have focused on the shining sea, the supreme skyline, the magnificent mountains, the shadow of the shoreline and the colorful clouds. Jesus, however, saw a few men of whom the world would say were the least likely to succeed. Jesus saw some Galilean fishermen. He looked at them. He perceived them. Jesus took note of them.

As Jesus walked by the Sea of Galilee, He saw the two brothers Simon and Andrew. He looked at them and didn't see what the world said they were: poor, useless fishermen. He looked at them and saw what He knew they could and would become, world changers.

We walk by this world's sea of humanity every day, but we often fail to slow down long enough to notice the people of humanity. We are all busy and often distracted. We have places to be and deadlines to meet. Could it be that God the Holy Spirit could prompt you along the way to actually stop and see the person right in front of you? Jesus' first step to *speaking the language of the fishermen* was to *see the fishermen*.

You live where you live, work where you work, and attend school where you attend school for a reason. Are you seeing the people who God has put in your life? Are you paying attention to the people who God has placed in your path?

In Matthew 4:18, the Bible says that upon seeing the fishermen,

Jesus "said to them." Jesus didn't speak about them. He didn't speak at them. The Son of God didn't speak over or above them. He spoke to them. Jesus was self-aware. He knew exactly who He was, and He knows exactly who He is. Yet, the Creator of the world didn't consider Himself too important to stop and speak to these two fishermen.

Who do we think we are? Why do we think so highly of ourselves? Aren't we in desperate need of some healthy self-awareness? We put way too much authority into what we think about ourselves. In fact, if you are submitting to the authority of what you think, you stink! Because submitting to the authority of what we think always stinks! We may think we are too important to speak to certain people, but Jesus reminds us we are never too important to stop and speak to people! Open your mouth and speak to people!

Jesus Spoke Into the Fishermen's Lives

Jesus saw the fishermen on the Sea of Galilee. He spoke to them. Furthermore, He spoke into the fishermen's lives as He met them right where they were.

In Matthew 4:19, Jesus said "Follow me, and I will make you fishers of men." Jesus noticed the fishermen were fishing; therefore, he spoke their language. Simon, Peter, James and John were not fishing for recreation. Fishing was their livelihood. Hence, Jesus spoke into their lives using the language they spoke: the language of fishermen.

Jesus told them He would make them "fishers of men." Jesus didn't tell these fishermen that He would make them accountants of men, bankers of men, doctors of men, engineers of men, lawyers of men or Youtubers of men (At a recent 5th grade awards ceremony, the number one most popular occupation 5th graders desired to pursue after college was that of a Youtuber). Jesus met these fishermen right where they were while they were fishing, and He spoke their language.

Based upon Matthew 4:18, Jesus didn't call Simon and Peter when they were cleaning fish, eating fish, loading their fishing boat, or unloading fish from the boat; but Jesus called them specifically while they were *casting a net into the sea*. Likewise, Matthew 4:21 tells us that Jesus called James and John while they were doing the specific task of *mending their nets.*

Is there any significance to *what* the disciples were doing *when* Jesus called them? Yes! Robby Gallaty describes the significance of casting and mending nets:

> In Jesus' day, fishermen cast their nets repeatedly into the water to catch fish. They tossed a circular net measuring about twenty feet in diameter, weighed down by heavy bars of metal or rocks attached to the edges. Tossing it away in a circular motion, the goal was to land it like a parachute in the water. As the net descended to the bottom of the lake, the fish swimming below it would be trapped in the netting. The fishermen would then dive out of the boat, swim to the bottom, gather the weights, and drag the entire net back to the boat or onto the shore. As you can imagine, this process was laborious and repetitive, and there were no guarantees that they would catch anything. But that didn't diminish the importance of casting the net. The only way to catch fish was to continually cast the net, throwing it out again and again, time after time....**Ministry with Jesus is exactly the same way. He has called us to cast the net, but he's responsible for the catch. We cast; he catches**....After a long night of fishing, James and John were busy in the boat with their father, engaged in the loathsome practice of repairing their nets. A torn net was as useless to a fishermen as a boat without a sail to a sailor....The

same word **(mend)** is also found in Ephesians 4:11-
12…to equip **(or mend)** the saints for the work of
ministry (emphasis mine).[25]

Jesus could have called these fishermen at any time, but He called them at a very specific time for a very significant reason. The disciples *casting* the net has a direct correlation to personal evangelism, while *mending* the nets is a picture of discipleship. Gallaty added, "He (Jesus) was preparing them for their future profession of *casting* for the lost and *equipping* the saints."[26] Jesus spoke at just the right time for the disciples to understand that their responsibility would be to *cast* for people, not *catch* people.

Jesus, the gospel conversationalist, has called us to be *casters*, not *catchers*. Too many pastors and churches, however, are asking the wrong questions. Two questions often asked of and by pastors are as follows:

(1) *"How many is your church running?"*
(2) *"How many is your church catching?"*

Two better questions pastors and churches should be asking are:

(1) *"How many in your church are fishing?*
(2) *"How many in your church are teaching others to fish?"*

Being "fishers of men" who make "fishers of men" means Jesus will not ask us how many we *caught* but He will ask us how many we *taught*. Let's not lose sight of being "gospel conversationalists" who make "gospel conversationalists."

Tonya and I are the blessed parents of two girls. Tonya doesn't like to fish, neither does our oldest daughter Braydee. Belle, our youngest, loves to fish. Though allergic to fish, I love teaching her how to fish. Teaching Belle how to cast her bait-casting reel is one of the joys of being her dad. Watching her make her first cast was just as rewarding as seeing her catch her first bass. Fishing is fun, but teaching Belle how to fish is rewarding. Who are you teaching to fish for people? Though you may be allergic to sharing your faith, God expects you to teach others to share their faith. Who are you teaching to fish for people?

Further evidence of Jesus speaking the fishermen's language is seen not only in *what* the disciples were doing when Jesus called them, but *where* they were when called. At the beginning of Jesus' earthly ministry, He called His disciples *from* Galilee. At the end of His earthly ministry, Jesus called His disciples back *to* Galilee.

Matthew 28 records Jesus' message to His disciples that they would see Him in Galilee. Specifically, in Matthew 28:10, the Bible says, "go and tell my brothers to go to Galilee, and there they will see me." When the disciples went back to Galilee, they saw the resurrected Jesus.

Why did Jesus call them back to Galilee? Why not Jerusalem, Jericho, or Samaria? Why Galilee? Jesus was speaking their language! He knew that the disciples would be familiar with Galilee. Galilee was the place where Jesus first spoke to the fishermen and spoke into their lives. Before Jesus ascended to the Father, Galilee would be the place where Jesus would begin to speak through the fishermen.

Jesus Spoke Through the Fishermen

Fishing trips don't always go as planned. Perhaps you have experienced more than one fishing trip like this one. The temperature in the air and in the water couldn't be more perfect for catching fish. The bait selection is the right choice for that time of year. The weather and the wind couldn't be more cooperative. Your casting couldn't be more spot-on as you masterfully pinpoint each cast. Everything may be going just right on your fishing outing with only one exception: the fish are not interested. Sometimes fish don't open their mouths. Of all the great fishermen who have ever fished, none of them have ever been able to open a fish's mouth. Not even Jonah was able to open the great fish's mouth to get out!

As fishermen of men, we are never called to open the hearts of people to be saved by the gospel. But, we are called to open our mouths to share the gospel. By opening our mouths to share the gospel, we are making ourselves available. When we make ourselves available, the Holy Spirit speaks through us. Jesus was teaching His disciples this timeless truth just before He ascended, as recorded in Matthew 28.

Jesus' first and last words to His disciples were similar. Matthew 4:19 records Jesus' first words to His disciples as He called them: "I will make you fishers of men." Matthew 28:19 records Jesus' last words to His disciples as He commissioned them: "Go therefore and make disciples of all nations." Jesus called these fishermen to be made into "fishers of men." Then, He commissioned them to go make disciples. How is this call and commission different?

A helpful exercise in discerning the difference between Jesus' call to His disciples and commission of His disciples is to examine the grammatical mood of these two statements. In grammar, moods are forms of the verb that express how the action or event is presented by the speaker. Four different moods are found in Greek grammar: indicative, subjunctive, operative and imperative.

These four grammatical moods are not referring to moods we may have before, during, or after Starbucks. The indicative mood presents the action or event as an objective fact. For example, "The door is opened." The imperative mood expresses a command, such as "Shut the door!" The subjunctive mood describes a probable situation; for example, "The door may be opened." The operative mood identifies an obtainable wish as indicated by "I wish the door was opened."[27]

Jesus' call to His disciples, "I will make you fishers of men," was in the indicative mood, which is an objective fact. On the contrary, Jesus' commission of His disciples, "make disciples," was in the imperative mood, which is a command. In the Bible, indicatives tell us what has been or will be done, while imperatives tell us what we must do. Indicative moods are descriptive as they describe an action. Imperative moods are prescriptive as they prescribe an action. Indicatives are stated facts, and imperatives are commands.

Confusion in interpretation arises when we mistake indicatives for imperatives and imperatives for indicatives. Jesus' commissioning of the disciples found in Matthew 28 is not a description of a one-time isolated event. Rather, the Great Commission is a prescribed commission for every follower of Jesus in any and all generations.

Although we aren't always present in fulfilling the Great Commission, the good news is that Jesus is never absent from it. In Matthew 28:20, Jesus promised, "I will be with you always to the end of the age." Again, we see Jesus speaking the disciples' language as He knew they didn't want to be separated from Him. Jesus promises all of His disciples that as we make ourselves available to make disciples who make disciples, He will always be with us.

Jesus spoke to the fishermen. Jesus spoke into their lives. Jesus promised them that He would speak through them. Jesus still speaks through His disciples! What do we have to fear? Put your faith into action and fulfill the Great Commission! Remember, it takes more faith to fear than it does to be faithful. Fear is simply putting faith in the enemy, while faith is putting confidence in Jesus!

From the time He called them until the time He commissioned them, Jesus spoke the fishermen's language. Haddon Robinson provided a helpful illustration that reminds us of the power of speaking a person's language:

> I am told several years ago a high-rise hotel was built in Galveston, Texas, overlooking the Gulf of Mexico. In fact, they sank pilings into the gulf and built the structure out over the water. When the hotel was about to have its grand opening, someone thought, *What if people decide to fish out the hotel windows?* So they placed signs in the hotel rooms,

"No fishing out the hotel windows." Many people ignored the signs, however, and it created a difficult problem. Lines got snarled. People in the dining room saw fish flapping against the picture windows. The manager of the hotel solved it all by taking down those little signs. No one checks into a hotel room thinking about fishing out of the windows.[28]

I concur. No one who is checking into a hotel is thinking about getting into his or her room in order to fish out of the window. The language written on those "no fishing" signs was powerful enough to persuade people to fish in spite of the signs verbiage.

When we take the time to speak to a person in a way that will connect with them, to speak their language, it is powerful. A gospel conversationalist will be like the original gospel conversationalist, Jesus, and seek to speak a person's language. Don't only speak to people, but seek to speak his or her language!

Jesus Spoke the Crowd's Language

"Lifting up his eyes, then, and **seeing that a large crowd was coming toward him**, Jesus said to Philip, **'Where are we to buy bread, so that these people may eat?'** He said this to test him, for he himself knew what he would do. Philip answered him, 'Two hundred denarii would not buy enough bread for each of them to get a little.' One of his disciples, Andrew, Simon Peter's brother, said to him, 'There is a boy here who has five barley loaves and two fish, but what are they for so many?' Jesus said, 'Have the people sit down.' Now there was much grass in that place. So the men sat down, about five thousand in number. Jesus then took the loaves, and when he had given thanks, he distributed them to those who were seated. So also the fish, as much as they wanted. And when they had eaten their full, he told his disciples, 'Gather up the leftover fragments, that nothing may be lost.' So they gathered them up and filled twelve baskets with fragments from the five barley loaves left by those who had eaten. **When the people saw the**

> **sign that he had done, they said, 'This is indeed the Prophet who is to come into the world!'"**
>
> **John 6:5-14**

> **"Jesus said to them, 'I am the bread of life; whoever comes to me shall not hunger and whoever believes in me shall never thirst.'"**
>
> **John 6:35**

Jesus Saw the Crowd

Crowds can be finicky. Jackie Robinson was the first African American to play major league baseball. While breaking baseball's "color barrier," he faced jeering crowds in every stadium. While playing one day in his home stadium in Brooklyn, he committed an error. His own fans began to ridicule him. He stood at second base, humiliated, while the fans jeered.

Shortstop "Pee Wee" Reese came over and stood next to him. He put his arm around Jackie Robison and faced the crowd. The fans grew quiet. Robinson later said that arm around his shoulder saved his career.[29]

Jesus faced some finicky crowds. When Jesus entered Jerusalem, at the beginning of the week of His crucifixion, the crowd was cheering, but at the end of that same week the crowd was jeering. Another particular crowd was ready to coronate Jesus as their King, but soon, many of them walked away and no longer followed Him. John 6 recorded the account of Jesus feeding this finicky crowd.

The miracle of Jesus feeding the five thousand is the only miracle, besides the resurrection of Jesus, which appears in all four gospels. John's gospel offers an important detail of this miracle. Jesus asked His disciples where they would get enough food to feed the five thousand.

Andrew, Simon Peter's brother, was the disciple who often

brought people to Jesus. In John 6:9, Andrew brought a little boy, who had two fish and five loaves, to Jesus. Jesus transformed this little boy's Arabic Appetizer into the Bible's Bottomless Brunch Buffet, the Christ's Combo, the Chosen One's Choose 2, the Disciples' Denarius Menu, God the Father's Filet-O-Fish, Fish-fil-A's Fish-n-Minis, the Holy Spirit's Half-&-Half, Little Tiberius Caesar's Hot-&-Ready, Heaven's 7-count, the King of Kings Kids Meal, the Palestinian Pick-2, the Lake of Tiberias' Lunchable, the Lord of Lord's Lunchbucket, the Master's McMuffin, the Sea of Galilee Sliders and the Son of God's Snack Pack. Jesus multiplied this little boy's Hebrew Happy Meal and fed five thousand men plus women and children. As the original gospel conversationalist, the Lord Jesus used this miracle to speak the language of the crowd in order to have a gospel conversation.

In John 6:5, the Bible says that Jesus was, "seeing that a large crowd was coming toward him." The Greek word for "seeing" means "to attentively notice," "to look at," and "to observe."[30] Jesus took note of the large crowd coming toward him. He looked at them. He observed them. Jesus paid attention to the crowd. He had compassion on them.

Jesus didn't take notice of the crowd in order to avoid them. Our 21st century American society is geared toward avoiding the crowds. Whether it be self-checkout lines, interstate bypasses, theme park fast passes, online shopping, online banking, online networking or social media, our society goes to great lengths to avoid great crowds. We rarely look at a crowd with compassion; rather, we look at a crowd with contempt. Oh Lord, forgive us!

Erwin Lutzer has said:

> In the storms of life sometimes we can't see God,
> but I want you to know that that is not nearly as
> important as the fact that God sees us.[31]

Jesus saw this hungry crowd and knew they had nothing to eat.

Daniel Goleman's description of empathy is an accurate picture of what Jesus saw when He saw the crowd:

> Empathy is used in three distinct senses: *knowing* another person's feelings, *feeling* what that person feels, and *responding* compassionately to another's distress. In short, I notice you, I feel with you, so I act to help you.[32]

Jesus' empathy extended past the crowd as He sought to involve his disciples in providing enough food for this crowd.

The disciples, however, didn't have the same amount of empathy as did Jesus. Philip observed that even if they had enough money to buy food for such a crowd, which they didn't, there would be nowhere to buy bread at that hour.

In Mark 6:36, Mark's account of this event, the disciples tell Jesus to "send them away to go into the surrounding countryside and villages and buy themselves something to eat." In essence, the disciples' counsel was to tell the people to "Get your own food!" Simon Baron-Cohen has pointed out that "people do not have the same amount of empathy."[33] Obviously, the disciples' empathy was far less than that of Jesus.

Why did Jesus' first disciples have to struggle to be as compassionate as Jesus? Why do we? Oswald and Jacobson offer a helpful insight:

> The term "to have compassion" (*splagchnizomai*), which refers to a sensation in the innards, regarded as the seat of emotions, is used many times in the Gospels and, as an emotional response to the plight of another, can probably be equated with what we now call empathy. This word was not used metaphorically for "compassion" or "pity" in Greek literature, but it is found in late Jewish literature (in

Greek) to designate *specifically divine compassion.*
The word occurs only in the synoptic Gospels in
the New Testament and is used primarily of Jesus.[34]

How can we express the same amount of empathy as Jesus? The Holy
Spirit helps believers see people as Jesus sees them.

In seeing the crowd, Jesus also saw His disciples. He didn't see
one at the expense of the other. Oswald and Jacobson explain the
abundance of Jesus' empathy well:

> The most spectacular demonstration of God's
> abundant care, of course, is the story of the feeding
> of the multitudes....Confronted with huge crowds
> that had come together in a desolate place, the
> disciples wanted to send the people away to towns
> where they might find food. Jesus asked what food
> people in the crowd had with them and was told of a
> boy who had two dried fish and five loaves of bread.
> "But what are they among so many?" the disciples
> asked. Jesus knew something the disciples did
> not: that God, beyond providing merely enough,
> would in fact provide an abundance—food for the
> multitude, plus twelve baskets more.[35]

Jesus provided enough for the crowd and His twelve disciples. This
is further evidence that Jesus compassionately saw both the crowd
and His disciples.

As believers, what can we do to increase our empathy and see
people as Jesus saw them? How can we see people with compassion
and not with contempt?

Give something away daily. Steve Gaines inspired this first
step toward seeing people as our Savior sees people. Gaines shared
that one of his goals is to give something away every day. He seeks
to practice generosity daily.[36]

We are most like God when we give. Our God is a giving God. Each day, let's seek to give something away, and it doesn't have to be money. Get creative with what you give away. We can give away our place in line, a prayer, a compliment, a word of encouragement, a Scripture verse, a testimony, the gospel, or anything else the Holy Spirit gives you to give away. Simply ask the Holy Spirit, "What would You have me give away today?" Remember, what you give away never goes away! God will use it now and for eternity.

As a pastor, I have tried to teach our church staff the importance of what the Bible says in Acts 20:35, "It is more blessed to give than to receive." Each time we go out for a staff lunch, I remind them that based upon Acts 20:35, they will be blessed if they pay for my lunch. So far, they have all forfeited that blessing. Seriously, let's seek to give something away daily.

Go out of your way weekly. I love my weekly routine. In fact, if my routine gets messed up, then I am not pleasant to be around. The more I read the Gospels, however, the more I am reminded that Jesus was often interrupted. Often times, Jesus' practice was to go out of His way.

In today's digital world, most places of business have access to the internet. Go out of your way once a week by taking your office out of the office. One day a week, study or work at a neighborhood coffee shop. Coffee shops provide a place where people are accustomed to engaging people in conversation. Go out of your way weekly by setting up shop in a coffee shop!

Get out of your comfort zone monthly. A gospel conversationalist becomes comfortable at being uncomfortable. In 2 Corinthians 1:3, the apostle Paul wrote, "Praise be to the God and Father of our Lord Jesus Christ, the Father of compassion and the God of all comfort." God is the God of all comfort, but God doesn't comfort us to make us comfortable. God comforts us so that we can comfort others. God's comfort came to you with the purpose of going to someone else.

Set a goal of getting out of your comfort zone monthly. The only time many believers ever get out of their comfort zone is on a mission trip once a year. We can do better than that! Think about ways you can serve your city or community that is out of your comfort zone. Take some time monthly and go serve at a jail, nursing home, children's home, or a homeless shelter. Jesus saw the crowd with compassion, not contempt. So should we.

The Crowd Saw What Jesus Did

Despite all of the sinful people in the crowd, Jesus saw the crowd with compassion. Likewise, when the people saw what Jesus did, they were ready to crown Him as king. Crowds of people can cause people to respond to different situations in various ways.

Forty members of our church traveled to the Billy Graham Training Center at the Cove for a retreat. On the way back to Chattanooga, our group stopped to eat at Cracker Barrel. We were sure to call the restaurant ahead of time to let them know that a party of forty was on the way.

When we arrived they were ready for us as they lined us up against the wall next to the candy. Lining up forty Southern Baptists beside a wall of candy is dangerous! I was standing at the podium waiting for our group to be seated. We weren't able to sit together as one group, so they sat us down in groups of four to six per table. The hostess was seating one table at a time, one right after the other.

Meanwhile, the regular lunch crowd line began to back up. Two lines formed; our line and the regular lunch line. Another hostess came and sat a young couple waiting in the regular line. Behind that young couple was an older couple.

After our hostess sat most of our group, the husband of this older couple began to verbally attack her. "How many people in this tour group are you going to seat before you start seating us? Our money is just as good as their money! We are paying customers just like they are! Why aren't you seating us?" He was irate!

The hostess said, "Sir, we will seat you as soon as we can. They were here first." He responded, "How do you know they were here first?" As the shepherd of the sheep, I walked closer to him and said, "Sir, they are seating both our group and the lunch crowd." He said, "I work in food service and this is not how this works!"

Our last group was being seated, and I was on my way to the table. On the way, the Holy Spirit moved me to stop. I stopped! I sensed the Spirit telling me to go and pay for the man and his wife's lunch. I said, "Lord, he doesn't deserve for me to pay for his meal." The Holy Spirit said, "Sam, when has whether or not a person deserves it ever been a pre-requisite or a qualifier/disqualifier for grace? The very fact that he doesn't deserve it is the very reason why you are going to pay for his meal!" I said, "Yes, sir!"

God didn't' speak to me audibly. Yet, even if He had, I wouldn't have been able to hear it because the irate man was yelling at his server. At this point, the man is standing at his table while his wife is seated. The server is waiting for the man to be seated, but he is too angry to sit. I am waiting on the server, so I can pay for the couple's meal. The husband was so angry that he told his wife to get up and they stormed out. He forfeited the grace that could have been his.

Too many people are as bitter, jealous, fearful, prideful, lustful, and ungrateful as this man was angry. Far too many people are forfeiting the grace that could be theirs by walking away from an opportunity to see Jesus.

In John 6:66, the Bible says that "many of his disciples turned back and no longer followed him." Not everyone in the crowd who saw Jesus feed the multitude believed and followed Him. Even Jesus, the original gospel conversationalist, had people walk away from the grace only He offers.

As gospel conversationalists, we must remember that we are not the point, but we are the pointers who are to point people to Jesus. We must never make our gospel conversations about us or for us, but about Jesus and for Jesus! When we enter gospel conversations, we must remember that we are not merely transferring information about us. Rather, we are informing people of the transformation that has taken place in us because of Jesus. On either side of the Great Commission is an exhortation of Jesus' power, that He has "all authority," and Jesus' presence, that He will "be with us to the end of the age." These two bookends help us remember that we are not the point of gospel conversations, but we are the pointers pointing people to Jesus!

Any and every conversation counts because any and every conversation matters. As gospel conversationalists, our goal is to steer any and every conversation away from ourselves and toward Jesus. We want the crowds to see Jesus, not us. Let's show the crowds what has happened in us and to us, so the crowds can see Jesus! How can we shape our conversations in such a way to point people to Jesus?

Pat attention to pronouns. Is your gospel conversation saturated with first person personal pronouns like me, my and I? Are you your biggest fan? Do you like to tweet, post, text and talk about yourself? Pay attention to the next tweet, post, text or conversation you have and make note of the number of times you use a first person pronoun to refer to yourself.

In order to point people to Jesus, we need to decrease the amount of time we spend talking about ourselves. Limit the use of first person personal pronouns while sharing your testimony. Sure, your testimony is your testimony, but fine-tune your story by highlighting God's story. Be careful not to glamorize your sinful life before you came to Christ while minimizing Jesus' saving grace.

Listen to the lost. In 2 John 9, the Bible says, "Everyone who goes on ahead and does not abide in the teaching of Christ, does not have God." Those who *do not have God* are like Kate, John Locke, Sayid, Claire, Charlie, Jack, Hugo, Shannon, James, Boone, Mr. Ecko, Desmond, Libby and Walt, they are LOST! Lost people act like lost people. The most effective way you can connect to a lost person is to listen. Listen to his or her story. Listen to his or her heart. Listen to the lost.

Speak the Scriptures. Our words will save no one, but God's Word will save anyone. When having conversations, be sure to speak the Scriptures. The best way to connect with someone may not be to quote the Scripture in King James language while giving a Scripture reference. But, an effective way to connect with people will be to drop sections of Scripture in your conversation smoothly. For example, "Jesus came to this earth to give us life now and forever." Or, "God loves you so much that He sent His Son Jesus to die in your place."

Jesus Spoke the Language of the Crowd

The South East Asia crowd that gathered at the train station that 2003 July morning was massive. Tonya and I were ready to take our weekend mission to Rangoon, Myanmar. Our mission was to drop Bibles in the Burmese language (which was illegal to have in our possession) out of the window of the train at each stop along the twelve-hour trip.

Upon arriving at the train station, we received news that our train was delayed. The 6:00 a.m. departure time was replaced with a 6:00 p.m. departure. Finally, after a twelve-hour delay, just before 6:00 p.m., we boarded the train. Our seats were in the first class section, which only meant that our seats were cushioned. The ordinary class seats were a single wooden bench that stretched from one end of the car to the other. While the lower class was just an empty car where people piled in and sat on the floor.

As the train pulled away from the station, immediately, we recognized a problem with accomplishing our mission. Two Myanmar military guards with automatic weapons were stationed on our car, one at the front and one at the back. We had one big bag full of five hundred Burmese Bibles, which was illegal. With these guards watching us, there was no way we would ever be able to drop them out of the windows. The first two hours we sat in frustration, unable to drop the Bibles.

The train was a boxcar World War II type of train that raced across the tracks at speeds of fifteen to twenty miles per hour. As the slow-moving train rocked from one side to the other across the tracks, people began to fall asleep, including the two Myanmar military guards. Just a few hours into our trip, Tonya and I were the only two people awake. We were so excited that we could now start dropping the Bibles out of the window.

Every twenty minutes or so, the train would slow to a stop and people would get off and others would get on. For twelve hours, each time the train stopped and before it took off again, we would drop several Bibles out of the window. By the time we reached our destination, the bag of Bibles was empty. We accomplished our mission!

The next leg of our journey was to cross a river that would take us to our hotel where we would stay for the next two nights. Since our train was delayed twelve hours, we missed the river ferry and had to wait another eight hours for the next ferry. About six hours into our eight-hour wait, we noticed a few men with small, motorized boats offering to take people across the river. We paid the fare and jumped in only to be bombarded with one of the most violent downpours of rain we have ever experienced.

After crossing the river, we took a Myanmar version of a rickshaw to our hotel. I will never forget falling back on that hotel bed, exhausted, soaking wet, thirsty, hungry, and frustrated after a thirty-plus long hour trip. In the middle of my pity party, as I was complaining to God, He spoke to me louder than if He had spoken audibly.

The Lord brought back a prayer that the Myanmar missionary prayed before Tonya and I left on this mission:

> Lord, open the eyes of the people who need to see these Bibles being dropped and close the eyes of the people who don't need to see them being dropped.

God said plainly to me:

Sam, I purposely delayed that train twelve hours because I knew that the people on the train would fall asleep as it traveled at night. By them falling asleep, you were able to drop the Bibles out the window. Sam, this is not about you! This is about Me getting My Word to the Burmese people in their language! Sam, this is your last chance to answer My call to vocational ministry. You choose this day whom you will serve, yourself or Me.

That moment was *the* moment when I surrendered to God's call on my life for vocational ministry. By getting those Burmese Bibles to the Burmese people, God was able to speak the language of the crowds in Myanmar.

After feeding the multitude, Jesus spoke the language of the crowd. The people were searching for Jesus because of the temporary satisfaction they received from the fish and loaves. Jesus, however, took advantage of the miracle and used it to speak the crowd's language. We read in John 6:35, "Jesus said to them, 'I am the bread of life; whoever comes to me shall not hunger and whoever believes in me shall never thirst.'"

Jesus didn't tell this crowd that He was the "light" or the "resurrection." He told them that He was the "bread of life." Why? Jesus knew they had bread on their mind, but He wanted them to have the "bread of life" in their hearts. Jesus spoke the crowd's language!

Jesus Spoke Nicodemus's Language

"Now there was a man of the Pharisees named Nicodemus, a ruler of the Jews. **This man came to Jesus by night and said to him, 'Rabbi, we know that you are a teacher come from God, for no one can do these signs that you do unless God is with him.'** Jesus answered him, 'Truly, truly, I say to you, unless one is born again he cannot see the kingdom of God.' Nicodemus said to him, 'How can a man be born when he is old? Can he enter a second time into his mother's womb and be born?' Jesus answered, 'Truly, truly I say to you, unless one is born of water and the Spirit, he cannot enter the kingdom of God. That which is born of the flesh is flesh, and that which is born of the Spirit is spirit. **Do not marvel that I said to you, You must be born again.** The wind blows where it wishes, and you hear its sound, but you do not know where it comes from or where it goes. So it is with everyone who is born of the Spirit.' Nicodemus said to him, 'How can these things be?' Jesus answered him, '**Are you the teacher of Israel and yet you do not**

understand these things? Truly, truly, I say to you, we speak of what we know, and bear witness to what we have seen, but you do not receive our testimony. If I have told you earthly things and you do not believe, how can you believe if I tell you heavenly things? No one has ascended into heaven except he who descended from heaven, the Son of Man. And as **Moses lifted up the serpent in the wilderness, so must the Son of Man be lifted up, that whoever believes in him may have eternal life.'"**

John 3:1-15

Nicodemus Thought Much of Jesus

Two researches with the National Study of Youth and Religion at the University of North Carolina at Chapel Hill interviewed over 3,000 teenagers about their religious beliefs and have recorded their findings. The social scientists summed up the teens' beliefs as listed below:

(1) **A god exists who created and ordered the world and watches over human life on Earth.**

(2) **God wants people to be good, nice, and fair to each other, as taught in the Bible and by most world religions.**

(3) **The central goal of life is to be happy and feel good about oneself.**

(4) **God does not need to be particularly involved in one's life except when God is needed to resolve a problem.**

(5) **Good people go to heaven when they die.**

Even these secular researchers acknowledged that the teens' beliefs were a far cry from Christianity with no place for sin, judgment, salvation, or Christ. On the contrary, many teenagers believe in good works, psychological well-being, and a distant god. Such a belief system has been defined as "Moralistic Therapeutic Deism."[37]

A close cousin to Moralistic Therapeutic Deism is what some refer to as Cultural Christianity. David Platt spoke to the reality of Cultural Christianity:

> There are a whole lot of people in our country who think they are Christians but they are not. Many Americans culturally identify themselves as Christians and biblically are not followers of Christ.[38]

Cultural Christianity has a shallow a view of Jesus, if any view of Jesus at all. Dean Inserra said:

> If you live in the South, there's a good chance your biggest mission field is people who have grown up in a culture where you can be a Christian without Jesus.[39]

Nicodemus was such a person, that is, one who grew up in a culture of religion (Judaism) without Jesus. Nicodemus thought much of Jesus, but he didn't think *enough* of Jesus. Nicodemus recognized that Jesus must be from God, but he didn't go so far as to recognize that Jesus is God.

For my pastor friends, church leaders, and followers of Jesus who serve in the South, this chapter may be the most important in this whole book. Why? Nicodemus is an example of a modern-day cultural Christian (whether a pastor, leader, or churchgoer) who does not know Jesus as Savior. Jesus' conversation with Nicodemus provides helpful insights for sharing Christ with those deceived by Cultural Christianity.

Nick was curious at night. Nicodemus approached Jesus

at night. He thought enough of Jesus to approach him with his curiosity. Why at night? Was nighttime the normal time for such a visit? Was Nicodemus fearful to approach Jesus during the day? Did he approach Jesus at night to avoid the crowds? The Holy Spirit doesn't tell us *why* Nicodemus visited Jesus at night, but He does share with us *what* this night visit entailed.

Nicodemus was representative of the best in the nation of Israel. He was a teacher of the Law, a Pharisee and a member of the Jewish ruling council also known as the Sanhedrin. The men of the Sanhedrin were the religious decision-makers and experts in all things religion. As an expert in the Law, men like Nicodemus didn't waste their time talking to just anybody. Nicodemus, however, thought enough of Jesus to approach Him and talk to Him teacher to teacher. As a fellow teacher, Nicodemus believed he wasn't wasting his time talking with Jesus. This ruler of the Jews observed that God must be with Jesus because of the miraculous signs He was able to do. Yet, Jesus was on a higher level than Nicodemus. God was not merely with Jesus, Jesus is God!

Jesus fed off of the curiosity of Nicodemus by quickly redirecting his thoughts. In John 3:3 and 6, Jesus tells Nicodemus that he "must be born again" and "that which is born of the Spirit is spirit." Jesus, being from above, was not on the same level as Nicodemus. Nicodemus, therefore, needed to be born from above. He needed to be spiritually transformed from death to life, from darkness to light and from being physically born to being spiritually born again. We were born to be born again! Go tell your Nicodemus that we were all born to be born again!

Nick was serious at night. However sinister the nightlife in Jerusalem was and regardless of all the nightlife opportunities, Nicodemus was serious about seeking out Jesus. After Nicodemus heard that he was born to be born again, he inquired about the meaning of what Jesus said. Nicodemus didn't believe that Jesus was referring to reincarnation or a second physical birth, but he didn't understand what Jesus meant by being born again.

As serious as Nicodemus was to understand what Jesus was saying, his lack of understanding was difficult to overcome. He understood and spoke the cultural, religious lingo, but he failed to understand that Jesus *is* the eternal "BINGO!"

What can we glean from Nicodemus thinking much of Jesus, but not thinking enough of Jesus? How can we apply what we learn from Jesus' conversation with Nicodemus to reach modern-day cultural Christians with the gospel?

Be understandable. Seek to understand more than seeking to be understood. If we are going to reach folks in the South, then we must understand that Cultural Christianity is alive and well. Also, we must recognize the cultural beliefs that are mistaken as Christian. Four common erroneous beliefs about Christianity that are prevalent in the South are as follows:

(1) **Christianity is a political party.** Far too many people in the South believe and behave as if Christianity is synonymous with a political party. Just like the Sanhedrin was not the Christian faith in Nicodemus' day, no political party is the Christian faith today.

(2) **Christianity is about being good.** Christianity is not about being good, it is about God. The Christian faith is not a list of rules to follow. Christianity is not the good –'ole-boys club, it is the new-in-Christ church. We need to remind people who are convinced that being good is the way to God that we are unable to get to God on our own. Faith alone in Jesus alone by grace alone is our only hope of ever getting to God!

(3) **Christianity is an SEC Country thing.** Jesus was not a blue-eyed, blonde-headed, white-skinned American. Similarly, Christianity is not only for people who grew up in SEC country. Sure, Jesus is the only way for people in SEC country to be saved, but He is also the only way for anyone, anywhere to be saved. Just because you were born in the

buckle of the Bible Belt never means that you are a default Christian. Remember, you were born to be born again.

(4) **Christianity is about living off my parents' faith.** Christianity is not about living off the faith of your parents. The only places in Scripture where we are told that Jesus *marveled* centered around people's faith or lack thereof. More specifically, Jesus *marveled* when those who had no business believing (Gentiles) believed. Likewise, Jesus *marveled* when those who had every reason to believe (Jews) failed to believe. More and more children who grew up in churchgoing homes are walking away from the church as they get older. Is Jesus marveling at those who grew up in church, but then walk away? As we seek to have gospel conversations, we must call these confused cultural Christians to personally place their faith in Jesus and stop relying on the faith of their parents.[40]

Be approachable. Jesus is an equal opportunity Savior. A quick survey of the four Gospels only further cements the truth that Jesus was the most approachable person to ever walk the earth. Jesus was approached by the demoniac and demons, sinners, and tax collectors, Pharisees and Sadducees, Jews and Gentiles, slave and free, rich and poor, well and sick, men and women, boys and girls.

Jesus remained approachable even to the point of death. On the cross, Jesus was approached in a conversation by a criminal. This criminal recognized who Jesus was and who he was in light of the Christ. Upon humbling himself and confessing his guilt, the criminal asked Jesus to remember him when He came into His kingdom. Jesus told him that on that very day he would be with Him in paradise. Even in His most uncomfortable, vulnerable state, hanging on the tree, soaking the cross in His own blood, breathing His last, Jesus remained approachable.

Why are we so opposed to being approached? Again, who do we think we are that we can't be approachable? How can we avoid being uncomfortably approached when our Savior lived and died that very way for us? Why do we look past the person we are talking with to see if there is another person who may be less awkward or more important?

I am blessed to serve as a pastor in the South. Yet, I know the struggle of preaching the gospel every week, giving an invitation to which no one responds. I, too, struggle with the temptation of wanting to be in an unreached, unengaged place where lost are saved every week; however, I am quickly reminded that people in the South need the gospel, too. God has called me to open my mouth and share the gospel with people in the South. Southerners are caught on the merry-go-round of Cultural Christianity and they need Jesus as their personal Savior! Let's follow our Savior and remain approachable!

Be teachable. We read in John 3:10 that Jesus referred to Nicodemus as "the teacher of Israel." Israel's teacher had much to learn. Primarily, Nicodemus learned that he was not Israel's true teacher, but Jesus was the Teacher of Israel. Nicodemus could have easily shrugged Jesus off. He could of walked away not allowing himself to be teachable; however, Nicodemus remained teachable.

How important it is for gospel conversationalists to remain teachable. As Israel's teacher, Nicodemus was the mouthpiece for the people of Israel, but he knew he had more to learn. Jesus came to teach Israel's teacher that he was missing it altogether. Sure, he had a head-knowledge of Scripture, but Nicodemus was missing the whole point of the Scripture. He thought the message of the Scripture was *"you must try again"* when in reality the message has always been *"you must be born again."*

Believe it or not, we don't know all things. We barely know anything at all. One of the greatest pulpiteers ever to expound the Scriptures, W. A. Criswell, said it this way:

> After seventy years of expository preaching, I have
> yet to touch the hem of His garment.[41]

The leaders of tomorrow are readers today. You never learn enough to stop being teachable. Remain teachable by learning various gospel conversation strategies, reading, studying, listening to preaching, and journaling through the Word.

Jesus Taught Nicodemus Much

Jesus spoke Nicodemus' language by using the language found in the Torah. Nicodemus, the teacher of Israel, would have been very familiar with the Law and writings of Moses. Jesus, then, used an account from the days of Moses to connect Nicodemus to Himself as the Savior of Israel and the world.

In John 3:13, Jesus told Nicodemus, "No one has ascended into heaven except he who descended from heaven, the Son of Man." Jesus was explaining to Nicodemus that He was then, and is now, the "Ladder" between heaven and earth. Furthermore, in order for Nicodemus to be "born again," he must put his faith alone in Jesus alone as his Savior.

In keeping with the thought of elevation to heaven, in John 3:14, Jesus spoke of the time when "Moses lifted up the serpent in the wilderness." Jesus went on to say in John 3:14-15, "so must the Son of Man be lifted up, so that whoever believes in him may have eternal life." Jesus spoke to Nicodemus in a way that he could understand. Jesus spoke Nicodemus' language.

How did Jesus speak Nicodemus' language? Nicodemus would have been keenly aware of the account of Moses lifting up the serpent in the wilderness. God's people were complaining about being led into the desert to die. So, God sent serpents into their camp and anyone who was bitten, died. Then, the people confessed their sins against God and asked Moses to ask God to take the snakes away. God told Moses to make a bronze serpent, put it on a pole, lift up the pole and whoever was bitten by a snake could look at the serpent and be healed.

Jesus used this account of Moses to help Nicodemus understand that Jesus is the One who will die on a pole and be lifted up to save any and all who trust in Him. What Jesus said to Nicodemus would not have connected with the Samaritan woman, the rich young ruler or with Zacchaeus, but it did connect with Nicodemus. Jesus spoke Nicodemus' language! As gospel conversationalists we must seek to speak the language of the people with whom we are speaking.

The gospel of Jesus informs the lost they're lost. Lost people come in different shapes, sizes, and flavors, but they are all lost. Some lost people are mean. Other lost people are nice. Some lost people are rich. Other lost people are poor. Some lost people look like us while other lost people don't. At some time, all lost people are unaware of their lostness. Most of the time, lost people are lost unaware.

As gospel conversationalists, especially in the cultural Christian climate of the South, we must be aware that lost people are lost, and many of them don't even know it. We have all heard the ol' preacher say, "We gotta get 'em lost before we can get 'em saved!" The truth in that statement lies in the fact that the lost are lost unaware. While traveling, some people, when they get lost, may not stop to ask for directions, but most all lost travelers are aware of being lost. Sometimes, our first step is helping people see they are lost without Christ.

The gospel of Jesus transforms the lost. Nicodemus, the Samaritan woman, Zacchaeus, and the rich young ruler were all lost. Jesus connected with each of these individuals in a different way but with the same hope. Jesus is the only way to be saved, but there are many ways to Jesus. Be sensitive to the leading of the Holy Spirit to help you discover the best way to steer a conversation to the Lord Jesus! Pray and ask God to help you see the right time to steer your next gospel conversation to Jesus.

Jesus Spoke the Samaritan Woman's Language

"A woman from Samaria came to draw water. Jesus said to her, 'Give me a drink.' (For his disciples had gone into the city to buy food). **The Samaritan woman said to him, 'How is it that you, a Jew, ask for a drink from me, a woman of Samaria?' (For Jews have no dealings with Samaritans).** Jesus answered her, 'If you knew the gift of God, and who it is that is saying to you, 'Give me a drink,'' you would have asked him, and he would have given you living water.' The woman said to him, 'Sir, you have nothing to draw water with, and the well is deep.** Where do you get that living water? Are you greater than our father Jacob? He gave us the well and drank from it himself, as did his sons and his livestock.' Jesus said to her, 'Everyone who drinks of this water will be thirsty again, but whoever drinks of the water that I will give him will never be thirsty again. The water that I will give him will become in him a spring of water welling up to eternal life.'** The woman said to him, 'Sir, give me this water, so that I will not be thirsty or have to come here to draw water.' Jesus said to her, **'Go, call your husband and come here.' The woman answered him, 'I have no husband.' Jesus said to her, 'You are right in saying, I have no husband; for you have had five husbands, and the one you have now is not your husband**. What you have said is true.' The woman said to him, 'Sir, I perceive that you are a prophet. Our fathers worshiped on this mountain, but you say that in Jerusalem is the place where people ought to worship.' Jesus said to her, 'Woman, believe me, the hour is coming when neither on this mountain nor in Jerusalem will you worship the Father. You worship what you do not know; we worship what we know, for salvation is from the Jews. But the hour is coming, and is now here, when the true worshipers will worship the Father in spirit and truth, for the Father is seeking such people to worship him. God is spirit, and those who worship him must worship in spirit and truth.' The woman said to him, 'I know that Messiah is coming (he who is called Christ). When he comes, he will tell us all things.'"

John 4:7-26

"Jesus said to her, 'I who speak to you am he.' So the woman left her water jar and went away into town and said to the people, 'Come, see a man who told me all that I ever did. Can this be the Christ?' They went out of the town and were coming to him."

John 4:29-30

Jesus Had Something to Say to the Woman

We all have personal preferences and pet peeves. One of my pet peeves is seeing able-bodied people who are riding in those motorized Walmart carts. You know: the cart with the basket on the front, the handlebar behind the basket, running boards on the bottom for your feet and a seat on the back of the cart. I am more apt to sit on the judgment seat when I see an able-bodied person sitting on a Walmart motorized cart seat. As long as I am able, I have vowed never to sit on a motorized Walmart cart seat.

As I pulled into the Walmart Neighborhood Market parking lot, I saw a sweet little elderly lady wrestling to unload her groceries from her Walmart motorized cart. Clearly, this lady was a perfect, legit candidate for the usage of a motorized cart. She had her walking cane in the basket, and she was struggling to pivot from the cart to put her groceries in her car. At one point I just knew she was about to fall.

Racing across the parking lot to help her, I asked, "Ma'am, may I help you with your groceries?" She responded, "No, thank you, I just loaded the last bag." I reached over into the basket and took her walking cane and handed it to her. Then, she said, "Well, you could help me by returning this cart back into the store so I don't have to make the trip." How could I say no to that? "Yes ma'am!" She sincerely said, "Thank you."

There I was standing next to this cart. I have one hand on the handlebars and one hand on the back of the seat trying to push the cart. It won't budge. I begin to think to myself, "Is the battery dead? No. Will it go forward? No. Will it go backward? No." I tried pushing it forward and backward to no avail. For one to two minutes I am trying to get this cart to move. Yet, this cart is having no part of moving.

By this time, the sweet elderly lady has made her way back around the car and said, "Are you having trouble?" In a tone of frustration, I blurted out, "I can't get this cart to move." With a look only a grandmother could give, she said, "Oh, son, the cart won't move unless you are sitting on the seat. You have to sit on the seat for it to move." Me? Sit on this seat? No way! At this point, I decided, I am going to wait until she drives off, and I will go get a Walmart employee to get the cart.

Then, looking directly at me, the lady said, "Now, I am going to stand here and not leave until you return that cart back into the store. Someone else may need to use it." I reluctantly said, "Yes ma'am."

I, an able-bodied grown man, sat down on that Walmart motorized cart and drove it through the parking lot back to the store. The speed of that cart was slower than Blobby the Blob's motorized scooter in *Hotel Transylvania 2*. I had one foot on the ground trying to kick it along. All the while, people were driving by staring at me, judging me. By the way, I don't judge them for judging me. In fact, I would have judged me, too.

Upon arriving at the front of the store, I noticed a Walmart employee standing outside the store on her break. I said to her, "I am returning this cart for an elderly lady." The employee, not believing a word I said, looked at me and gave me an, "Mmmm. Hmmm. You are too kind."

In 1 Corinthians 9:22, Paul wrote, "I have become all things to all people, that by all means I might save some." I never thought that I would forsake one of my pet peeves, riding a motorized cart while able-bodied, in order to connect with this sweet lady and engage her in a conversation.

Jesus was the Master at becoming all things to all people to save some. He engaged people in different ways. Forsaking all the cultural pet peeves of a Jewish male, Jesus engaged the Samaritan at the well.

Jesus never had to say something. Rather, Jesus always had something to say. He had something to say to the Samaritan woman. For the sake of the Samaritan woman and her city, it was good that Jesus had something to say to her.

Besides, Jesus' disciples weren't going to enter into a conversation with the Samaritan woman for two reasons. First, the disciples would have none of it because Jews had no dealings with Samaritans. Second, it was the noon hour, which meant it was time to eat. The disciples went into the city to buy some food. Jesus' disciples were not focused on the Samaritan woman's spiritual thirst because they were hungry. Some things never change. Too many followers of Jesus in the twenty-first century, when hearing this text preached on a Sunday morning, are counting down the minutes to the noon hour. Disciples got to eat! Throughout history, how many disciples have failed to offer the living water to the spiritual thirsty because they are focused on their physical hunger? How many times have I failed to do so? What about you? God help us!

Meanwhile, this woman of Samaria came to the well at noon in order to draw water. Most of the women of Samaria drew water in the morning, but this particular woman came later because she was an outcast even in her own community. Certainly, she was the talk of the town and considered to be one of the worst of sinners. Her reputation was the polar opposite of Nicodemus' reputation.

The Samaritan woman was not dumbfounded that people talked about her, but she was floored when Jesus talked to her. Her own words captured her sheer shock, "How is it that you a Jew ask for a drink from me, a woman of Samaria?" What's more, she wasn't bowled over by what Jesus *asked of her*. Yet, she was baffled by Jesus *asking her*, one of the most sinful thought of women in all of Samaria. By Jesus speaking to her, He was breaking down cultural, racial, social, religious, gender, and generational barriers.

Be a gospel, not a gossip, conversationalist. Jesus had something to say *to the woman*, not *about the woman*. Plenty of other people were gossip conversationalists, but Jesus was and is the original gospel conversationalist. Jesus knew everything about the Samaritan woman, even the sin that was hidden in her heart. Yet, Jesus didn't gossip about her, He shared the gospel with her.

As followers of Jesus, we are called to be gospel conversationalists.

The world doesn't need any more gossip, but people are thirsting to hear the gospel. Let's stop sharing gossip about people, and let's start sharing the gospel with people. Let's stop having to say something about people, and let's start saying something to people.

Jesus Had Something to Say about Water

In regards to His encounter with the Samaritan woman, Jesus *had* something to say about water. Jesus didn't engage the woman at the well in a conversation about Moses lifting up a pole in the wilderness. He didn't engage her in conversation about fishing, money, resurrection, nor Him being the bread of life. By engaging her in a conversation about water, Jesus was speaking the Samaritan woman's language. She was familiar with water.

Jesus noticed that every day this woman hauled her water jar to Jacob's well to draw water. The mundane, everyday chore of fetching her jar and drawing water became the avenue by which Jesus shared the gospel. Masterfully, Jesus began the conversation by *asking her for help*, not by *telling her how she needed help*. How important it is to start a gospel conversation by *inquiring of a person* in order to hear from them, rather than *interrupting or ignoring a person* to be heard by them.

Jesus was sitting beside Jacob's well. The Samaritan woman came to the well because she and her household were thirsty. Jesus, the Living Water, told the woman that everyone, including Jacob of whom the well was named, who drank the water Jesus gives will never thirst again.

Immediately, the Samaritan woman wanted Jesus to give her the water of which He spoke. She wanted to be satisfied. She didn't want to be thirsty anymore. She didn't want to feel she had to draw water from the well at noon: all the other Samaritan women went to the well earlier in the day, but to avoid ridicule from the other women the Samaritan woman went at noon. She was tired of the shame, humiliation, and guilt. She jumped at the chance to never have to be shamed by visiting the well at noon. She visited the well at noon to avoid being shamed.

Upon her interest in receiving the water that wells up to eternal life, Jesus pointed the Samaritan woman back to her sin. Jesus asked her to go get her husband. By doing so, Jesus zeroed in on her thirst for loved and value. Spiritually, Jesus was the One she was trying to find in all five failed marriages. She confessed she had no husband. Jesus affirmed her response and went on to tell her everything she had ever done, including her current situation.

Be a gospel, not a Google, conversationalist. You don't have to be an expert of many things to share the main thing. You don't have to be like Google and share expertise in many things; be like God in the flesh, Jesus, and share the main thing. Search for common ground, make a connection and share the gospel.

Jesus could have sat the Samaritan woman down and dazzled her with His infinite knowledge of H2O: where it came from, why it runs downhill, why it's wet. Jesus could have entered into a discourse on the ins and outs of the three states of water: liquid, solid and gas. He could have introduced the idea of bottling water and made the Samaritan woman the wealthiest person in the known world. But, Jesus was interested in using a conversation about water to show this woman her life of sin and the reality of her need for salvation.

God, the Creator, created creation. All of creation screams that there is a Creator. Human beings were created in the Creator's image. Therefore, any and everything in all creation can be used to start a gospel conversation, even water. Nothing in all creation is too significant, nor too insignificant to use to start a conversation about the gospel of Jesus Christ. As gospel conversationalists, we need to remember that Jesus still has something to say about water. In your next gospel conversation, look for the "water" the Holy Spirit will use to guide your conversation to the gospel!

Jesus Had Something to Say About Worship

The Samaritan woman recognized that Jesus was more than just a Jewish man passing through Samaria. She referred to Him as a prophet. Rather than confessing her sin and repenting of her sinfulness, she decided to deflect to a longstanding worship war. Apparently, worship wars were around long before the Southern Baptist Convention.

Jesus didn't blink. He embraced the opportunity to say something about worship, because Jesus has something to say. Whether in the context of water or worship, Jesus had something to say to the Samaritan woman. Jesus' audience analysis was second to none. He knew *what* to say, *how* to say it, and *when* to say it. As gospel conversationalists, what can we learn from Jesus' conversation with the Samaritan woman concerning worship?

We are all wired to worship. We were all created to worship. Jesus told the Samaritan woman that the Samaritans were worshiping what they didn't know, but the Jews were worshiping what they knew. What's more, Jesus told her that salvation comes from the Jews. What did Jesus mean? Jesus, the Savior of all, was a Jew born of the seed of Abraham. Hence, the Savior who provides the only salvation came from the Jews.

Also, Jesus never one time argued that Samaritans or Jews were not worshiping. All of mankind was created to worship. Although the object of our worship may be different, we are all wired to worship. The first two people who were created, Adam and Eve, worshiped God as they walked with Him in the cool of the day.

A gospel conversationalist will take advantage of the glorious truth that we are all worshiping something. We just need to be able to point people to worship Jesus and nothing else. In your next gospel conversation, ask the Holy Spirit to help you discern who or what that person is worshiping. Most people talk about and get excited about what is close to their heart. Use that to point the person to the One who is worthy of worship, Jesus!

Where we worship matters. The Samaritan woman brought up that Samaritans say the place of worship is *here* but the Jews say the place of worship is *there*. Many gospel conversations never get off the ground because people argue about the place of worship. Some say, "I can worship in a deer stand or on the lake just as well as in a church." In defense of not attending a corporate place of worship, others say, "I love Jesus, but I can't stand the church."

Jesus told the Samaritan woman the time is now that we are to worship the Father in spirit and truth. Now is the time to stop the ageless, countless, endless, fruitless, hopeless, loveless, meaningless, mindless, pointless bickering about when or where we are to worship. We should worship the Lord anywhere, anytime and anyplace. Worshiping the Lord should happen at home, school, work, and even at church! As you have gospel conversations, seek not to argue about the *when* or *where* of worship, but seek to agree on the *who* of worship!

Who we worship matters. Samaritans only accepted the first five books of the Old Testament and outright rejected the rest. Moreover, they flat out dismissed Isaiah's Suffering Servant, the Psalmist's "the Lord is my shepherd" and all the Old Testament prophecies of a soon-coming Messiah. Today, either by way of ignorance, arrogance, or defiance, many people do not know Jesus, much less that He is worthy of their worship.

As gospel conversationalists, we need to be cognizant of the fact that far too many people don't even know that God created them and that He loves them. We are responsible for telling them that Jesus made them, loves them, lived for them, died in their place, and was raised from the dead for them! The world, your world, needs to know that who we worship matters!

How we worship matters. Jesus told the Samaritan woman that God the Father is seeking true worshipers who worship in spirit and truth. We are not to worship in spirit *or* truth, as if we get to pick one. We must worship in spirit *and* truth.

To worship in spirit requires that one be born of the spirit by way of the Holy Spirit. Some gospel conversations stall when a person says, "I have always known Jesus!" Wrong! That is like saying, "I have always been born physically!" Just as there was a point in time when one is born physically, there must be a point in time whereby one is born spiritually. People need to be reminded that just like they have not always been alive physically, neither have they always been alive spiritually.

To worship in truth means to be grounded in the Word of God. The Bible is truth. Read the Word. Pray the Word. Journal through the Word. Memorize the Word. Believe the Word. Live the Word. Share the Word. Speak the Word. Love the Word. Listen to the Word. Respond to the Word. Be hearers and doers of the Word. In your next gospel conversation, ask the Holy Spirit to prompt you to speak the Word as He leads.

John Piper wrote about the balance of worshiping in spirit and truth:

> Worship must be vital and real in the heart, and worship must rest on a true perception of God. There must be spirit and there must be truth. Truth without emotion produces dead orthodoxy and a church full (or half-full) of artificial admirers. On the other hand, emotion without truth produces empty frenzy and cultivates shallow people who refuse the discipline of rigorous thought.[42]

Why we worship matters. Jesus told the Samaritan woman that God is seeking true worshipers. We worship because God is seeking worshipers! God sought you out when you were lost. God sent His Son to this earth to seek the lost. God will send His Son to this earth again to retrieve His bride, the church.

It is time to worship! Jesus has come and He is coming! Jesus could split the sky at any moment! Are you ready? Will you be found worshiping? Jesus' coming is soon; it is sure, and it will be seen! As gospel conversationalists, we must allow this truth to ignite a fire of urgency in our hearts to have gospel conversations! Let's be like Jesus and speak the truth by speaking the language of the people with whom we are speaking.

Jesus Spoke the Rich Young Man's Language

"And behold, **a man came up to him, saying, 'Teacher, what good deed must I do to have eternal life?'** And he said to him, 'Why do you ask me about what is good? There is only one who is good. **If you would enter life, keep the commandments.'** He said to him, 'Which ones?' **And Jesus said, 'You shall not murder, You shall not commit adultery, You shall not steal, You shall not bear false witness, Honor your father and mother, and, 'You shall love your neighbor as yourself.'** The young man said to him, 'All these I have kept. What do I still lack?' Jesus said to him, **'If you would be perfect, go, sell what you possess and give to the poor, and you will have treasure in heaven;** and come, follow me.' When the young man heard this he went away sorrowful, for he had great possessions. And Jesus said to his disciples, **'Truly, I say to you, only with difficulty will a rich person enter the kingdom of heaven. Again I tell you, it is easier for a camel to go through the eye of a needle than for a rich person to enter the**

> **kingdom of God.'** When the disciples heard this, they were greatly astonished, saying, '**Who then can be saved?'** But Jesus looked at them and said, '**With man this is impossible, but with God all things are possible.'"**

Matthew 19:16-26

It's Hard to Go to Heaven

While serving as pastor in a previous church, the youth pastor and I had an opportunity to meet with two Mormon missionaries who were canvassing our community. We agreed to listen to what they believed as long as they would listen to a presentation of the gospel. We were excited about this opportunity to have a gospel conversation.

As they walked through their beliefs, we followed along in a pamphlet they provided. This Mormon magazine began with an explanation of the spirit world and then walked through the creation of creation. Jesus' life, death, burial and resurrection were almost lost in the busyness of the brochure. Finally, we got to the end of the booklet, and that's when I noticed it; hell was missing!

The very last page of the leaflet was a diagram of the three levels of heaven, but no hell. According to Mormon doctrine, even unrepentant sinners will go to heaven, albeit the lower level of heaven. Elaborating on this hellish doctrine, the two Mormons told us that how a person lives his or her life determines his or her level of heaven. Ultimately, they believe that almost everybody goes to heaven.

Of course, I inquired about what happened to hell. The two missionaries gave the same response, "Well, it's hard to go to hell." Again I asked, "What happened to hell?" And again they responded, "It's really hard to go to hell." I tried a different approach by asking, "Who is it that goes to hell?" Yet, again, they gave the same answer,

"It's really, really hard to go to hell." Exasperated I asked once more, "Well, does anybody ever go to hell?"

Reluctantly, they told us that the only people who will ever go to hell are those who join the church, the Mormon church, and then leave the church. Immediately, I blurted out:

> Wait a minute. If the only people who will ever go to hell are the people who join the Mormon church and then leave the Mormon church, then why are you trying to get us to join the Mormon church? If we are going to heaven anyway and the only way we would ever not go to heaven would be to join Mormonism and then leave Mormonism, then why are you putting our souls in jeopardy? If there is even the slightest chance that we would leave the Mormon church after joining, then why would you ever put our souls in jeopardy of going to hell?

Once more they answered, "But, it's hard to go to hell." In fact, the only response we ever got from both of them was simply, "It's really hard to go to hell."

Recognizing that hell is a terrifying subject helps us understand why the Mormon's attempt to erase it; however, our message must never be to *dismiss* hell, but to *miss* hell. Hell can't be erased, but it can be escaped by grace alone, through faith alone, in Christ alone.

According to the Lord Jesus, it is not hard to go to hell. On the contrary, it's hard to go to heaven. In a conversation with a rich young man, Jesus confirmed that it is not hard to go to hell, but it is really, really, really hard to go to heaven. In Matthew 7:13 and 14, Jesus said:

> Enter by the narrow gate. For the gate is wide and the way is *easy* that leads to destruction, and those who enter by it are many. For the gate is narrow

and the way is *hard* that leads to life, and those who find it are few.

He Asked the Right Person the Right Question

In Matthew 19:16-26, a rich young man approached Jesus and asked Him a question. In turn, Jesus entered into a gospel conversation with this wealthy young Jewish aristocrat. The man was rich, young, and most likely influential. He would have been the star on Judea's "Rich and Famous." He would have been the most eligible sought after bachelor on Judea's version of "The Bachelor."

In the Jewish culture of that time, people who were blessed financially, like this young man, were seen as those who had the favor of God on their life. Yet, something was missing. He had heard about Jesus' teachings, healings, and miraculous works. No doubt about it, this young man knew he was approaching the right person to get the answer that money couldn't buy. Or, could it?

Of all the questions he could have asked, this rich young man asked the right question. He didn't ask Jesus for personal healing, doctrinal clarification, relational reconciliation or some other miracle. He asked Jesus about what it takes to have eternal life. In the rich young man's mind, all Jesus had to do was tell him what to do and he would do it! He asked Jesus the right question.

A four-year-old boy was outside when a bee starting buzzing around him. Needless to say, he got upset, so his mom tried to calm him down.

> "Son, that bee is more afraid of you than you are of him," she said. Then she added, "Look how much bigger you are. Besides, if that bee stings you, his stinger will fall out and he will die."

The little boy thought for a few moments and then replied, "Does the bee know that?"[43]

Like this little boy, asking the right question is crucial. The next person with whom you engage in a gospel conversation may be asking important questions like:

- **How do I fix my marriage?**
- **Where can I find a job?**
- **How can I beat this addiction?**
- **Will I ever get married?**
- **How can I deal with this pain?**
- **Is there any hope for me?**

Certainly, these questions are important, but none of them should be considered *life's greatest question*.[44]

Rely on God's Word and the Holy Spirit. When you talk to people and they ask questions like the one's above, ask the Holy Spirit to help you steer them to begin contemplating life's greatest question. Ask the Holy Spirit to prompt you to ask the right questions that will lead a person to ask life's greatest question. All gospel conversationalists must rely on the power of the Word and the presence of the Holy Spirit! The rich young man asked Jesus the right question, life's greatest question.

He Got the "Write" Answer

In Matthew 19:17, Jesus gave the rich young man the "write" answer, "If you would enter life, keep the commandments." The "commandments" are referring to the Ten Commandments written by the hand of God, the Word of God. God's Word is not simply a good book; it's God's book! The written Word of God is always the write answer! Every gospel conversationalist must be sure that he or she is sitting under the preaching and teaching of the Bible. One has said, "Going to a church that doesn't teach or preach the Bible is like going to a restaurant that has no food."[45]

Far too many people are looking for eternal life in all the wrong places, while it can only be found in the "write" place, the Bible. The young man thought he could obtain eternal life on his own. In order for him to obtain it, then all he had to do was keep the Word of God perfectly. In Matthew 5:20, Jesus said, "For I tell you, unless your righteousness exceeds that of the scribes and Pharisees, you will never enter the kingdom of heaven." The only way to obtain eternal life on one's own is to be perfect in every way for a lifetime, which is impossible.

You know the "write" answer to give. Although the rich young man didn't know it, Jesus was his only hope. What's more, Jesus knew that the commandments were given to show all people their failure to obtain absolute goodness on their own. Like a surgeon's scalpel, the Word of God, which is sharper than any double-edged sword, lays open our innermost sin and exposes our wicked hearts. As a result, we are keenly aware of our need for someone else to save us from our sins.

A gospel conversationalist knows that Jesus is the only hope for anyone with whom he or she engages in conversation. You may feel like you don't have all the answers to engage someone in a gospel conversation. Perhaps you have thought:

- What if they ask me a question I am unable to answer?
- What if I freeze in fear?
- What if I can't think quick enough to give an answer?

As a follower of Jesus, you already know the "write" answer, the Bible! It's your responsibility to share the "write" answer, the written Word of God, while it is God's responsibility to save. The rich young man *got* the right answer because Jesus *gave* him the "write" answer. You give the "write" answer and the Holy Spirit will see to it that the person with whom you are engaging will get the right answer!

Jesus Met Him Right Where He Was

After the young man asked Jesus which commandments he should keep, Jesus mentioned five of the Ten. One of the Ten that Jesus didn't mention caught my attention. Jesus mentioned the fifth, sixth, seventh, eighth, and ninth commandment, but not the tenth. We read in Exodus 20:17, the tenth commandment, "You shall not covet your neighbor's house; you shall not covet your neighbor's wife, or his male servant, or his female servant, or his ox, or his donkey, or anything that is your neighbor's." Why didn't Jesus mention this commandment to the man?

The rich young man was rich. He could have anything he wanted. He was the neighbor whom the other neighbors were coveting. Jesus knew this man's heart. He knew that this man's fatal attraction was his own wealth, not someone else's wealth. Jesus knew what was keeping this rich young man from coming to Him. The Lord Jesus also knew what it would take to get him to follow Him.

Jesus knows what it takes to get people to follow Him. You don't have to know a person's heart in order to share the gospel. Jesus knows what is keeping people from Him and what it will take to get them to follow Him. Don't feel like you have to learn everything about a person in order to "earn the right" to share the gospel. Don't feel like you have to know the person's hidden sin so as to share the gospel effectively. Jesus knows every person inside and out. Make your next gospel appointment and point that person to Jesus!

He Knew He Wasn't All Right

Jesus spoke the rich young man's language. The approach Jesus took connected with the young man as evidenced by Matthew 19:20, "All these I have kept." The wealthy young Jew knew the Law, and he thought he kept the Law. Certainly, he too must have thought that the reason for God's favor on his life was tied directly to his own keeping of the Law. Jesus didn't engage the rich young man with the same language as He did Nicodemus, the Samaritan woman, the disciples, or even Zacchaeus. Jesus spoke language familiar to the young Jew.

Immediately, the wealthy aristocrat knew he wasn't alright, something was lacking. Inquiring about what was missing, he asked

Jesus, in Matthew 19:20, "What do I still lack?" Even the good Jew recognized that his perceived goodness wasn't enough. Religion was not satisfying him nor was anything else in the physical realm. Clearly, he was unsatisfied and unfulfilled.

How many people have you had conversations with that were unsatisfied and unfulfilled? On the outside, they have everything the American dream offers: a wife and children, a house, two cars in a two car garage, great job, and freedom to do whatever they want whenever they want. But, on the inside, they are miserable. Getting a person to the point where they know they are missing something more may take a number of gospel conversations. Be patient, but be persistent.

Jesus didn't leave the young man high and dry as He told him in Matthew 19:21, "If you would be perfect, go, sell what you possess and give to the poor, and you will have treasure in heaven; and come, follow me." Jesus called him to leave what he loved and follow Him. The rich young man's fatal attraction was his love of money, and Jesus pinpointed it.

What is keeping you from trusting in Jesus? Unlike the rich young man, we may not all be rich. But, like the rich young man, we all have fatal attractions that threaten our loyalty that is due the Lord Jesus. Although you may not know what it is, the next person with whom you share the gospel has a fatal attraction, that is, something that is keeping them from trusting in Jesus.

People can hear and fully understand the gospel, be drawn by the Holy Spirit, and even be asked to put their trust in Jesus; however, sometimes they don't make that life-changing decision because they know something in their lives will change. Furthermore, they are reluctant to put their faith in Jesus because of that which is keeping them from trusting in Jesus. Common responses may be "I am not ready yet" or "Let me think about it some more." In such a situation, two great questions to ask are, "What are you waiting for?" and "What is keeping you from putting your trust in Jesus right now?"

In his sermon, *Fatal Attraction*, Chuck Herring asked, "What is your fatal attraction?"[46] He offered the following options:

- **Is your fatal attraction your theology?** Do you think your perceived goodness is going to get you into heaven? Our perceived goodness is never good enough. Don't allow a flawed theology keep you from trusting in Jesus.
- **Is your fatal attraction your desire for pleasure?** Sin is fun for a time, a very short time. If you are having too much fun to follow Jesus, then you are playing on the devil's playground.
- **Is your fatal attraction your money?** Whether you have a little or a lot, the love of money is the fatal attraction of many. People who don't have money are busy trying to get it, while those who have it are busy trying to keep it. In your heart and life, don't allow the almighty dollar steal the loyalty due the Almighty God.

A gospel conversationalist will always look for ways to connect with a person by speaking his or her language. When you inquire about what is keeping a person from trusting in Jesus, ask the Holy Spirit to help you apply the gospel to that person's fatal attraction.

He Responded in the Wrong Way

Upon hearing Jesus' answer, the Bible says in Matthew 19:22, "He went away sorrowful, for he had great possession." The rich young man walked away. What caused him to walk away was not his allotment of money, but his love of money. Obviously, he responded in the wrong way. Walking away from Jesus is always the wrong way. When things don't go their way, far too many people go the wrong way and walk away from Jesus and His church.

Why is walking away from Jesus always the wrong way? Below are four reasons why walking away from Jesus is always the wrong way:

Jesus alone saves. For decades in the American culture of the South, it was enough to say, "Jesus saves." With the influx of different people groups from various parts of the world moving to the American South, it must now be said, "Jesus *alone* saves." Jesus is not one way among many other ways to be saved. He is not merely the best way to be saved. Jesus is not merely the most popular way to be saved in the South. He is the only way for anyone to be saved. We must tell people that Jesus alone saves!

Jesus alone still saves. Jesus is the Savior of those who believed in the past, believe in the present and will believe in the future. Today, the world is a hot mess and it is only getting messier. Truth is treated like a red-headed stepchild. Love is mistaken for hate, and hate is mistaken for love. Bad news has been dethroned by fake news. But, the good news is that Jesus alone *still* saves. We must tell people that Jesus alone *still* saves!

Jesus saves the unsaved. People are hoping without any hope. Many people are hoping in a lottery ticket, education, career, drugs, alcohol, success, prestige, reputation, or a new relationship. The only hope, confident assurance, we have in this life or the next is found in the Lord Jesus. We must tell people their only hope is Jesus!

Jesus is saving the saved. After coming to faith in Christ, people need to be taught how to grow in the faith. People need to know that God has given them His Word and the local church. New believers must be taught how to engage the Bible through reading, studying, journaling, memorizing, and sharing. Teaching new converts how to be disciples who make disciples is the work Jesus assigned. We can't afford to not be fishers of men who are making fishers of men. We must teach people that Jesus is saving the saved!

Jesus responded to the rich young man walking away. In fact, Jesus' own disciples were astonished at their Lord's reply in Matthew 19:23-24: "Truly, I say to you, only with difficulty will a rich person enter the kingdom of heaven. Again I tell you, it is easier for a camel to go through the eye of a needle than for a rich person to enter the kingdom of God." Jesus said what He meant, and He meant what He said.

If Jesus, the original gospel conversationalist, had someone walk away and reject Him, then don't lose heart when you share the gospel and people reject it. Pray for the person who rejects the gospel and ask God to give you another chance to share. Keep sharing the gospel. Keep praying to God. Keep trusting in the original gospel conversationalist!

Ultimately, Jesus made it clear that it's not hard to go to hell; rather, it's hard to go to heaven. Gospel conversationalists will be intelligently intentional about making it hard for people to miss heaven and dismiss hell! Don't shy away from conversations about heaven and hell. All of humanity will spend much more time in either heaven or hell than they will on earth. We need to tell people not to dismiss hell, but how they can miss hell!

Jesus Spoke Zaccheus' Language

"He entered Jericho and was passing through. And there was a man **named Zacchaeus. He was a chief tax collector and was rich.** And he was **seeking to see who Jesus was, but on account of the crowd he could not, because he was small of stature.** So **he ran on ahead and climbed up into a sycamore tree to see him,** for he was about to pass that way. And when Jesus came to the place, he looked up and said to him, **'Zacchaeus, hurry and come down, for I must stay at your house today.' So he hurried and came down and received him joyfully.** And when they saw it they all grumbled. **'He has gone in to be the guest of a man who is a sinner.'** And Zacchaeus stood and said to the Lord, **'Behold, Lord, the half of my goods I give to the poor. And if I have defrauded anyone of anything, I restore it fourfold.'** And Jesus said to him, **'Today, salvation has come to this house, since he also is a son of Abraham. For the Son of Man came to seek and to save the lost.'**

Luke 19:1-10

Jesus Had a Gospel Conversation with Zacchaeus

From the time our oldest daughter was born, Tonya and I have taken turns reading Bible passages to her before bedtime. One of the biblical accounts that I most enjoyed reading to her was Zacchaeus' encounter with Jesus. Of course, Luke 19:10 is the key verse in the book of Luke as it reveals Jesus' purpose for coming to this earth, which was to seek and to save the lost. However, that was not the reason I most enjoyed reading Luke 19:1-10 to Braydee. In fact, the reason was more practical than theological. Each time I would speak the name Zacchaeus, Braydee would turn her head around and give me a kiss on the cheek. Though she was too young to talk and tell me why she kept kissing me, I finally figured it out. When I spoke the name Zacchaeus, she heard the word "kiss." I was speaking Braydee's language.

Jesus spoke Zacchaeus' language. Wherever Jesus went, people came to faith in Him and began to follow Him. Whenever the gospel of Jesus is proclaimed, either through a conversation or preaching, someone will hear the gospel and may believe in Jesus alone, by grace alone, through faith alone. So it was when Jesus was passing through Jericho.

Zacchaeus heard that Jesus was passing through and had to see Him. The only problem was he was a short man and couldn't see over the crowd. He raced ahead and climbed a tree just to catch a glimpse of Jesus, but Jesus had other plans in mind. When Jesus arrived at the place where Zacchaeus was perched, He told him to come down. Jesus, knowing Zacchaeus wanted to see him, spoke Zacchaeus' language by telling him that He would stay at his house. Zacchaeus thought he was seeking Jesus, but in reality Jesus was seeking him.

Zacchaeus Became a Gospel Conversationalist

Jesus had a gospel conversation with Zacchaeus, which resulted in him becoming a gospel conversationalist. Do you have what it takes to become a gospel conversationalist? What does it take to become a gospel conversationalist? Zacchaeus' encounter with Jesus gives us eight characteristics of a gospel conversationalist.

1. See your sin. In Luke 19:10, we read, "He was a chief tax collector and was rich." Zacchaeus was an administrator of the Roman government's tax office. While reading this verse, I pictured Zacchaeus wearing a Statue of Liberty costume standing on the side of the road waving, jumping up and down, dancing, and flipping a Liberty Tax Service sign. What a special kind of person it takes to do that job during tax season! I almost feel like I need to repent, because I have never been that excited about tax season.

Other than what Luke 19:2 tells us, we know nothing more about Zacchaeus, but he knew more about himself. Zacchaeus saw his own sin. Being a chief tax collector meant that he was in charge of a number of other tax collectors. Zacchaeus was not rich because he won the lottery, inherited a ton of money or was named Zac Efron. He was rich because he overcharged the Jewish people on their taxes and took a cut for himself. His sin was not that he was rich but in the way he became and remained rich.

Unlike those who "grumbled" and said, "He has gone in to be the guest of a man who is a sinner," in verse 7, Zacchaeus saw his own sin. Those grumblers didn't see their own sins, but they did see Zacchaeus' sin. On the other hand, Zacchaeus was not seeing their sin or the sins of the crowd; he was seeing his own sin. A gospel conversationalist is one who sees his or her own sin. Are you seeing your own sin or someone else's?

Before you can own your sin and repent of it, you must see your sin. Don't allow your heart to get to the place of indifference about your own sin. Don't be like the man who asked the waiter for a coke and then proceeded to throw the coke in the waiter's face. The waiter was ready to fight, but the man apologized. He then asked for another coke. After promising he wouldn't shower the waiter with a coke again, the waiter reluctantly agreed to serve him another one. Again, the customer threw the coke in the waiter's face.

The man genuinely felt terrible about being unable to resist the urge to douse the waiter with coke. He checked himself into a clinic to go through some intense psychotherapy. Upon completing therapy, the man returned to the restaurant excited about the fact that he was healed.

He asked the same waiter for a coke in order to celebrate his recovery. The waiter wanted an assurance that the man was cured. He told him he was indeed cured. As quickly as the waiter handed the man a coke, the waiter was wearing the coke all over his face. The waiter exclaimed, "I thought you were cured!" The customer responded, "I am cured. I still have the compulsion, but I don't feel guilty about it anymore!"

We don't need to see our sin as merely a mistake, mishap, or misfortune. We must call our sin what it is: sin. Sin is evil. Sin is deadly. Sin is dangerous. Sin must be seen. Are you seeing your own sin?

2. Long to belong. Zacchaeus longed to belong. In verse three, the Bible says, "And he was seeking to see who Jesus was but on account of the crowd he could not, because he was small of stature." He couldn't see Jesus because of the crowd. Ouch! Have you ever considered that you are surrounded by modern day Zacchaeus's who long to belong?

We want to think the reason Zacchaeus couldn't see Jesus was because he was short, but the real problem was not his physical height, but the crowd's lack of spiritual depth. Sadly, no one in the crowd approached Zacchaeus and offered to put him on their shoulders. All around us are Zacchaeus's who are short in stature spiritually, emotionally, relationally, ethically, and theologically. Will you offer to come along side them and put them on your shoulders so they can see Jesus? Let's not be like the crowd and engage in gossip conversations; let's be like Jesus and be gospel conversationalists.

3. Become like a child. Zacchaeus was so ready to see Jesus that in verse 4, we read, "So he ran on ahead and climbed up into a sycamore tree." Being an influential, wealthy man of Eastern descent meant running was undignified, childish behavior. He was not just running, but he was running in the middle of a crowd. The fact that Zacchaeus was running is proof that he was becoming like a child.

Being of Western descent, most Americans do not consider running to be childish at all. What about climbing a tree? When was the last time you shimmied up a tree? If I were a betting Baptist, then I would bet that you haven't climbed a tree since childhood. Climbing a tree is certainly something that children love to do. Zacchaeus became like a child by running through the crowd and climbing a sycamore tree to see Jesus.

In Luke 18:17, Jesus said, "Truly, I say to you, whoever does not receive the kingdom of God like a child shall not enter it." As gospel conversationalists, we must be willing to go against what culture says and say what Christ says.

4. Be ready to respond. Zacchaeus was ready to respond. By Jesus stopping at the tree and telling Zacchaeus to come down, we know that Jesus knew who he was, where he was, and what he needed. Jesus knows who you are, where you are and what you need. Jesus knows who the person is whom you will engage in your next gospel conversation. He also knows where they are and what they need.

In Luke 19:5, Jesus tells Zacchaeus "Hurry and come down, for I must stay at your house today." What is glaringly obvious is the fact that Jesus didn't climb the tree to get the chief tax collector. Jesus didn't crank up a chainsaw and cut the tree down. What's more, Jesus didn't throw something in the tree to knock Jericho's tax assessor down. Zacchaeus took a step of faith and came down the tree to Jesus.

The phrase "received him joyfully," found in Luke 19:6, describes the manner in which Zacchaeus hurried down the tree to Jesus. The words "joyfully, gladly, rejoicing" appear nine times in the gospel of Luke to denote an attitude of joy accompanying faith and salvation.[47] Zacchaeus responded by grace alone, through faith alone, in Jesus alone.

Too many people believe they have to get their lives cleaned up before coming to Christ. Zacchaeus didn't tell Jesus, "Lord, you can't come to my house today, because I need to clean it up." Jesus cleaned up his house and his heart! Are you ready to respond? Are you ready to ask the next person you are in a gospel conversation with to respond?

5. Prepare to be persecuted. Gossips are going to gossip. Haters are going to hate. Persecutors are going to persecute. Grumblers are going to grumble. Rather than celebrating that Zacchaeus came to faith in Christ, these grumblers complained about Jesus eating with a sinner. As soon as Zacchaeus came to faith in Christ, the text says in verse seven, "And when they saw it, they all grumbled. He has gone in to be the guest of a man who is a sinner." No doubt about it, Zacchaeus was a sinner, but Jesus is the Savior!

Persecution comes in different ways, but persecution always comes. Gospel conversationalists need to be aware that persecution is real and relevant. Don't shy away from sharing the gospel because of persecution. Rejoice in the fact that by sharing the gospel you will also share in persecution.

6. Live for the Lord. How do we know if Zacchaeus was truly saved? He was saved because he was changed. Unlike the rich young man, who referred to Jesus as just a "teacher," Zacchaeus referred to Him as "Lord." In Luke 19:8, he said to Jesus, "Behold, Lord the half of my goods I give to the poor. And if I have defrauded anyone of anything, I restore it fourfold." Jericho's tax assessor is not talking to a teacher, he is living for the Lord!

By giving half of his possessions to the poor, Zacchaeus is not simply being a good man; he is a new man. Also, the four-fold restoration of those whom he defrauded is in obedience to the Law of Moses. No longer is Zacchaeus living by man's word; he is now living by God's Word. Be sure you are living for the Lord before you speak on behalf of the Lord!

7. Tell your testimony. Jesus quieted the grumblers quickly with His words in verse nine, "Today, salvation has come to this house, since he also is a son of Abraham." Jesus' statement was made to Zacchaeus, but it was directed to the grumblers. Is Jesus saying that the chief tax collector was saved because of his Jewish descent as a son of Abraham? Zacchaeus and Abraham were saved the same way, by faith. Therefore, this Jew from Jericho was saved because he was Abraham's spiritual descendent.

Can you imagine all the opportunities Zacchaeus had to share his testimony? Door to door he went through Jericho not taking money from people, but giving money back fourfold. The Jericho jaded were ready to hear from this former taker turned giver. What happened to him? Why is he giving back all this money? Rest assured, they were ready to hear about his heart change more than they were ready to receive monetary change. Who does God have ready to hear your testimony?

8. Call people to call on Jesus. As discussed in chapter II, sooner or later, a fisherman has to draw in the net that was cast. At some point, a gospel conversationalist has to call people to call on Jesus. Zacchaeus' testimony was simple, "While I thought I was seeking Jesus, Jesus came to seek me out and save me." Jesus called people to follow Him. Jesus called Zacchaeus to follow Him.

The word "today" in verse 9 of Luke 19 highlights the truth that gospel conversations are not seasonal; they can happen anywhere, anyplace and anytime. "Today" speaks of opportunity and emphasizes urgency. Gospel conversations must include a gospel presentation and a gospel invitation. We must invite people to invite Jesus into their life. We must call people to call on Jesus.

For 31 years Zeke the turtle lived securely in the home of Bob and Debbie Young. But on July 30, 2012, the box turtle escaped. Zeke was on the run for over a month. The couple put out fliers and ads as well as the utilization of search and rescue dogs trained to track down reptiles, but Zeke was never found.

One day the neighbor's golden retriever sniffed out Zeke as he was trying to hide in some ivy. Zeke's slow but steady month-long journey had taken him about 1,000 feet from the back door where he escaped. The neighbor said, "Zeke was just sitting in the yard waiting to be found."

Where is your Zeke? Where is your Zacchaeus? Your Zeke or Zach may be a great deal closer than you think. Even Zacchaeus is not too short nor is Zeke too slow to get lost in a crowd when Jesus is coming! In Christ, you do have what it takes to be a gospel conversationalist.

Jesus Spoke the Emmaus Road Travelers' Language

"That very day two of them were going to a village named Emmaus, about seven miles from Jerusalem, and they were talking with each other about all these things that had happened. While they were talking and discussing together, Jesus himself drew near and went with them. But their eyes were kept from recognizing him. And he said to them, 'What is the conversation that you are holding with each other as you walk?' And they stood still, looking sad. Then one of them, named Cleopas, answered him, 'Are you the only visitor to Jerusalem who does not know the things that have happened there in these days?' And he said to them, 'What things?' And they said to him, 'Concerning Jesus of Nazareth, a man who was a prophet mighty in deed and word before God and all the people, and how our chief priests and rulers delivered him up to be condemned to death, and crucified him. **But we had hoped that he was the one to redeem Israel.** Yes, and besides all this, it is now the third day since these things happened. Moreover, some women of our company amazed us. They were at the tomb early in the morning, and when they did not find his body, they came back saying that they had seen a vision of angels, who said that he was alive. Some of those who were with us went to the tomb and found it just as the women had said, but him they did not see.' And he said to them, 'O foolish ones, and slow of heart to believe all that the prophets have spoken! Was it not necessary that the Christ should suffer these things and enter into his glory?' And beginning with Moses and all the Prophets, he interpreted to them in all the Scriptures the things concerning himself. So they drew near to the village to which they were going. He acted as if he were going farther, but they urged him strongly saying, 'Stay with us, for it is toward evening and the day is now far spent.' So he went in to stay with them. When he was at table with them, he took the bread and blessed and broke it and gave it to them. And their eyes were opened, and they recognized him. And he vanished from their sight. They said to each other, **'Did not our heats burn within us while he talked to us on the road, while he opened to us the Scriptures?'** And they rose that same hour and returned to Jerusalem. And they found the eleven and those who were with them gathered together, saying, 'The Lord has risen indeed, and has appeared to Simon!' Then they told what had happened on the road, and how he was known to them in the breaking of the bread."

Luke 24:13-35

Jesus Reestablishes Hope

What is hope? Hope is the confident assurance of that which has yet to be realized. The very essence of hope is looking forward to something in the future. Hope focuses on the future, not the present or the past. The two travelers on the road to Emmaus made the following comment in Luke 24:21, "But we had hoped that he was the one to redeem Israel." Notice the word "hoped" is in the past tense. After the death of Jesus, hope was shattered. Did Jesus' death mean that hope was dead?

On the day of Jesus' resurrection, two of His disciples were on the road to Emmaus. While walking the seven-mile trip from Jerusalem to Emmaus, these two travelers were engaged in a gospel conversation. Discussing all that had taken place would have certainly included Jesus' erroneous arrest, the Pharisees plot, Jesus' traitorous trial, the crime at Calvary, reliable reports of Jesus' resurrection, and the undeniable empty tomb. Unbeknownst to them, the One whom they had hoped would redeem the nation hopped into their conversation.

When Jesus asked these two disciples what they were discussing, they were shocked. How could anyone in or around Jerusalem not be privy to the fact that Jesus of Nazareth was crucified? With tearful eyes and fretful faces, these disciples explained to Jesus how their hope was dead due to the death of Jesus. Then, reports of Jesus' resurrection ignited their hope again. Yet, when Jesus was not found at the empty tomb, their hope was dashed again. At this point, Jesus' disciples couldn't handle one more disappointment.

Are you at the point where you can't handle one more disappointment? If not, you certainly know someone who is at that point. We rub shoulders with people every day who are hopeless. People you know are suffering through a divorce, a death in the family, a health crisis, a financial collapse, job loss, or an addiction. When we encounter people who are disappointed with life, we must do what Jesus did. Jesus pointed these two hopeless disciples to Himself. We must be the pointers who point people to Jesus!

Jesus reestablished their hope by pointing them to Himself in the Old Testament scriptures. Jesus preached an expository sermon from Genesis through Malachi expounding all the Scriptures about Himself. In one question, Jesus unearthed their flawed theology. In Luke 24:26 Jesus asked, "Was it not necessary that the Christ should suffer these things and enter into his glory?"

The Jewish nation was under the impression that Messiah would come to militarily deliver Israel. Once Jesus died, before establishing His kingdom, the Jewish nation didn't recognize Him as Messiah. Jesus, however, came as the Suffering Servant, not a Militant Messiah. Jesus bore the gory cross before He wore the glory crown. Far too many people have the wrong understanding of Jesus' cross. What is the right understanding of Jesus' cross?

Christ was crucified. The cross of Christ means that Jesus died on the cross. Jesus' death was so public that the two travelers on the road to Emmaus were astonished that even a visitor had not heard about the public crucifixion. The Jews, the Romans, the crowds, and the disciples all witnessed the crucifixion of Jesus of Nazareth. Everyone in Jerusalem was aware that Jesus was crucified.

What about in your Jerusalem? Does everyone in your Jerusalem know that Jesus was crucified? Do they know that Jesus didn't die as some moral influence, to pay a ransom to the Devil, or to simply die a martyr's death? Do they know that Jesus died a substitutionary death? Do they know that Jesus died in their place and instead of them? If not, why have you not told them?

Sin was amplified. The cross of Christ means that sin was amplified. When we look at the cross we see what God thinks of our sin. We think our inner, hidden sin doesn't harm anyone; however, all sin hurts the heart of God. What we think of our sin doesn't match what God thinks of our sin. We consider our sin a small thing, but God sees our sin as *the thing* that sent His Son to the cross.

People need to know that our sin offends God. Yes, it may be offensive to tell someone his or her sin offends God, but it is offensive to God if we don't tell. An effective way to start a conversation about sin is to ask a person to define sin. Survey questions similar to these may be helpful: What is sin? Have you ever sinned? Is sin something you think about? Is sin something you talk about? When you sin, how does it make you feel?

God was satisfied. Who killed Jesus? What a timeless question! This timeless question has been asked for generations. Did the Romans kill Jesus? Did the Jews kill Jesus? Did the Gentiles kill Jesus? Did the Devil kill Jesus? Did your sin and mine kill Jesus?

In Isaiah 53:10, the Bible says, "Yet it was the will of the LORD to crush him." God the Father bruised His own Son on the cross. In fact, it pleased the Father to bruise Jesus on the bloodstained cross. Jesus voluntarily laid down His life to satisfy the wrath of God the Father. When Jesus said, "It is finished!" it's as if the Father said, "I am satisfied!"

Your family, friends, coworkers, and neighbors need to know that Jesus is enough to satisfy. If Jesus becoming sin for us was enough to satisfy God the Father, then Jesus' righteousness imputed to us by faith is more than enough to satisfy us. The same Jesus whose work of redemption satisfied God the Father is the same Jesus who satisfies sinners.

You and I are justified. When we look at the cross we should see that Christ was crucified, sin was amplified and God was satisfied; therefore, you and I can be justified. Each time we partake of the Lord's Supper we are remembering that through the cross of Jesus, God remembers our sins no more. In Christ, we are justified just as if we never sinned.

Too many people are looking for a Jesus who will relieve them of their sin rather than retrieve them from their sin. Jesus came to retrieve us from Hell's flock, not just to relieve us from Hell's flames. God the Son came to retrieve us from our bondage under sin, not just to relieve us with a bandage over our sin. People need to know that we will never be relieved from the presence and power of sin until we're first retrieved from the penalty of sin. Remind people that Christ will not do anything in us until we recognize that He has done everything for us in order to do something through us.

Jesus Reignites Hearts

By speaking the language of the Old Testament prophets, Jesus spoke the language of these two Jewish travelers. In Luke 24:25, Jesus mentioned how "slow of heart" they were "to believe all that the prophets had spoken." Jesus spoke the language that was written on their hearts, that is, the Old Testament. Upon hearing Jesus preach from Genesis to Malachi, their hearts were reignited. How are hearts ignited or reignited today?

Jesus, through the presence of the Holy Spirit, is the One who ignites and reignites hearts, not you or me. God is the One who is able to save; therefore, we are only required to be available to share. In order to share the gospel, a gospel conversationalist must deny self and rely on the Holy Spirit.

Denying self while relying on the Holy Spirit is counter-cultural. We live in a selfie society! What's more, we live in a fake selfie society because we take-a-selfie-multiple-times-until-we-get-the-best-pic-of-ourselves! In actuality, our fake selfie society is stealing our self-identity as we are tempted to present an inauthentic version of ourselves. The first step in denying self is to identify our true self. We will never deny self until we identify self. In personal evangelism, denying self means to make oneself available to share saving faith in Jesus. Once we deny self, then, we rely on the Holy Spirit and God's Word to save the person with whom we are sharing.

The Word of the Lord reveals the Lord of the Word. As gospel conversationalists, we must be consistent in saying what God says. Our words can change no one, but God's Word can change anyone. The world may be attractive to people, but God's Word is alive and active in people. Don't be ashamed of being unashamed of the gospel!

Jesus Is Recognized in the Humdrum

A good conviction for a gospel conversationalist is to keep it simple. Jesus was recognized in the mundane, humdrum, day-to-day experience of having a simple meal. Simply put, a gospel conversationalist doesn't need a huge evangelistic event to share the gospel. All we need is a simple prayer, a simple deed, a simple word, a simple smile, a simple meal, a simple Scripture, a simple conversation, a simple testimony, a simple gospel presentation and a simple gospel invitation.

Simply, open our eyes to Jesus' work. The work of redemption is complete. Jesus has done all the work to save. We are to be witnesses of His work and work as His witnesses. Let's open our eyes to Jesus' work and point others to do the same!

Simply, open our hearts to His Word. Working as Jesus' witnesses simply means to walk in His Word. The hearts of the two travelers on the road to Emmaus were stirred when Jesus began to expound the Word of God. Since God's Word has the power to open hearts, what can God do if we open our hearts to reading, hearing, memorizing and journaling through His Word?

Simply, open our mouths in this world. Working as Jesus' witnesses simply means we are to be witnesses in this world. Following Jesus means that we follow His approach to sharing the gospel. Jesus' approach was to open His mouth and speak the language of the people with whom He was speaking. We must do no less!

Jesus' Followers Must Speak People's Language

Tim was an intimidating-looking guy. He was tall and wore a long beard off his chin. He was bald and a bit rough around the edges. As I approached him, I asked the Holy Spirit to give me favor with Tim in hopes to share the gospel. Tim's youngest son was participating in our summer sports camp, which our church provides in support of a church plant in East St. Louis.

Tim was somewhat standoffish at first, but soon he warmed up to the idea of having a conversation. I asked a few get-to-know-you questions. He opened up and shared about his family situation. He was divorced, but he and his ex-wife remained good friends. Upon digging deeper, I discovered that Tim's oldest son with his ex-wife had died at the age of twenty. The reality of their son's death was devastating.

I prayed with Tim and told him we could talk the following day at camp. He agreed. The next day I noticed a necklace that Tim wore around his neck. It was quite unique. I had never seen a cross like the one dangling from his neck chain. He told me that it was a small urn, which contained his son's ashes. Immediately, the Holy Spirit prompted me to say:

Tim, thank you for sharing your son's story. I can't imagine what it must be like to experience the death of a child. Seeing your cross urn does remind me, however, of One who does know exactly what it is like to have a Son die, even to die on a cross. In fact, God the Father gave His Son, Jesus, to die on a cross for you and for me. Though I don't know how you feel, God knows exactly how you feel. God loves you and He gave His Son for you. Although Jesus died to pay the penalty for our sins, He didn't stay dead. He was raised from the dead; He is alive. By being raised to life, Jesus proves that He alone can forgive sin. If you repent of your sin and put your trust in Him, then you will experience life in the spirit now and life for eternity with Him in heaven.

The Holy Spirit granted me favor to speak Tim's language. Tim was all ears and listened intently and thanked me for sharing. He didn't trust Christ that day, but he heard the gospel in a way that spoke to him. Followers of Jesus must speak people's language. Why is it so important that we speak people's language?

People are lost. From the time people are born until they are born again, all people are lost. People of different nations are lost. Like the Samaritan woman, people in cities are lost. Like the rich young ruler, people with cash are lost. Like Zacchaeus, people in crowds are lost. Like Nicodemus, people in church are lost. People in homes are lost. We can never connect the wrong person to Jesus.

People are loved. God the Father loves people. He loves them so much that He gave His only Son. God the Son loves people. Jesus loves people so much that He came to seek and save them. God the Holy Spirit loves people. He loves people so much that He convinces them that Jesus is right and they are wrong. God's people must love people. People must be connected to the right person, Jesus.

People are looking. Unchurched people are looking. Churched people are looking. Unreached and unengaged people are looking. Even dechurched people are looking. People are looking for Jesus; they just don't know it.

People are longing. People are longing for something more. All over the world, including your next door neighbor, people are longing for joy and satisfaction. Your neighbors and all people everywhere need to hear that joy is only found in Jesus. What's more, God expects you to open your mouth and tell them.

Biblical joy is understood as a state of gladness in glad times, mad times, bad times, and sad times. Regardless of the circumstances, joy is the perpetual state of rejoicing. For those who put their faith in Jesus, He gives joy now. Also, Jesus gives complete and full joy in eternity. On earth, our joy in Jesus is tainted with sin, sorrow, separation, suffering, and sadness. In heaven, our joy in Jesus will be unadulterated. Hallelujah!

Our family made the decision to put in an in-ground swimming pool this summer. The pool company assured us that it would take them about seven days from start to finish. We were preparing for a summer full of pool parties. Unfortunately, three months into our pool construction, we had a hole in the ground with water in it but no concrete around our pool. Our pool was incomplete for three months. A myriad of reasons were given for why our pool remained incomplete.

Meanwhile, our girls enjoyed the incomplete pool over the summer. Although we were able to enjoy the pool, our enjoyment was incomplete. We often wondered if our pool would ever be complete; however, we also believed that when completed, our pool would be complete a great deal longer than it was incomplete. Our joy in our completed pool will overshadow our incomplete joy in our incomplete pool.

On a much higher scale, our incomplete joy in Jesus on earth will pale in comparison to our completed joy in Jesus in heaven. Again, hallelujah! People need to know about the joy they can have now and forever in Jesus. Will you go and tell?

People are listed. You know people. All of us have some type of contact list. Whether on a Rolodex or in our smart phone contacts, we all have people's contact information. How many of the people in your contacts have you conversed with about the gospel? How many of them have you told that they were born to be born again? How many of them have you talked to about the gospel? Make a list of people with whom God wants you to share the gospel. Pray for them. Ask God to give you a chance to have a gospel conversation with them? **See Appendix B.**

Jesus' approach to calling people to follow Him was simple.

> Jesus called people one conversation at a time. One conversation with blind Bartimaeus as he was begging, one conversation with a criminal on the cross while he was dying, one conversation with doubting Thomas as he was doubting, one conversation with His first disciples as they were fishing, one conversation with Martha as she was mourning, one conversation with Nicodemus at night, one conversation with Pilate before His punishment, one conversation with a rich young ruler as he was being ruled by his riches, one conversation with Saul the assassin as he was saved on the road to Damascus, one conversation with the woman at the well, one conversation with Zacchaeus in that sycamore's zenith, one conversation at a time.

Our approach to having gospel conversations should be the same as Jesus' approach, one conversation at a time. A gospel conversationalist is one who is working to win people to Jesus. May God grant you favor, boldness, opportunity and compassion as you work to win people to Jesus!

Appendix A

JOURNAL THROUGH THE WORD

"Turning Your Quiet Time into Quite a Time"

Has your quiet time been so quiet you haven't heard from God? **Journal through the WORD** is intentionally designed with the aim to turn your quiet time into quite a time with God.

"For the *word* of the LORD is upright." **Psalm 33:4.**

"I have stored up your *word* in my heart, that I might not sin against you." **Psalm 119:11.**

"Man shall not live on bread alone, but by every *word* that comes from the mouth of God." **Matthew 4:4.**

"Sanctify them in the truth, your *word* is truth. **John 17:17.**

"So Faith comes from hearing, and hearing through the *word* of Christ." **Romans 10:17.**

"Let the *word* of Christ dwell in you richly, teaching and admonishing one another in all wisdom." **Colossians 3:16.**

"For the *word* of God is living and active." **Hebrews 4:12.**

WORD is an acronym that stands for **Write, Observe, Reflect**, and **Do.** Three to five sentences, in each of these four sections, are sufficient to turn your quiet time into quite a time with God.

Write. As you journal through the WORD, begin by writing the word **Write.** As you read a passage of Scripture write out the words in a verse or the verse that jumps out at you. Include the following information in this section: the date, the name of the book, the chapter and verse reference, the verse, and title of the text.

Observe. As you continue to journal through the WORD, the second step is to write the word **Observe.** The goal here is to observe and discover the original meaning of the text by asking key questions about the text: Who is speaking? To whom are they speaking? Who wrote the text? What did the text mean then? When in the life of Jesus did this text take place? Did it take place before, during, or after the cross of Jesus? Why was the text written? How did people respond to the text back then?

Observe the type of genre in which the text is written. Is the text written as poetry, biography, narrative, parable, Law, history, wisdom, prophecy, discourse, letters, or proverbs?

Observe the grammatical nuances of the text in its context. Pay attention to the following: pronouns, repetitive words, shift in location, shift in speakers, shift in audiences, shift in thought, shift in subject, or shift in verbs.

Observe whether the text is written as a prescriptive text or a descriptive text. A **prescriptive text** is one that prescribes certain behaviors or actions. Prescriptive texts tell us "what to do" (commission) or "what not to do" (omission). A **descriptive text** is one that describes what is happening without giving commands or instructions on how to behave. Descriptive texts tell us "what happened."

Reflect. As you continue to journal through the WORD, the third step is to write the word **Reflect.** The goal here is to reflect and discover what the text means today. What is the meaning of this text today? What is the timeless truth of this text that transcends time? What is the take-a-way truth of this text?

Do. As you continue to journal through the WORD, the final step is to write the word **Do.** The goal here is to discover what God wants me to do in response to this text. What can I do to move me from a hearer of the Word to a doer of the Word? What application can be made from this text for my life today? In what ways does God want me to share His Word, pray His Word, memorize His Word, sing His Word, or obey His Word?

Sample WORD entry:

Write: Date: 8/15/16 Title: God Speaks: "So, faith comes from hearing, and hearing through the word of Christ." Romans 10:17

Observe: Paul is writing a letter to the followers of Christ in Rome. Romans is rich with the theology of salvation by grace. Paul is explaining how a person is saved in Romans 10. Paul is saying that the words or works of man can't save, but only God's redemptive work heard through His Word saves.

Reflect: God's Word must get into a person in order for them to be saved. Getting into God's Word allows God's Word to get into me. Getting into God's Word saves me and sanctifies me. Take-a-way Truth: Get into God's Word!

Do: Lord, help me to get into your Word daily. God wants me to set aside time each day to read His Word, hear His Word, pray His Word, and obey His Word.

Appendix B

LIST AND PRAY

List and pray for at least one person in your home:

_____

_____

List and pray for at least one person in your family:

_____

_____

List and pray for at least one person among your friends:

_____

_____

List and pray for at least one person among your social circles:

_____

_____

List and pray for at least one person at work or school:

_____

_____

List and pray for at least one person on your social media:

_____

_____

List and pray for at least one random encounter:

_____

_____

End Notes

1   Chris Lutes, *7 Reasons Not to Share Christ,* https://www.christianitytoday. com/iyf/hottopics/faithvalues/7-reasons-not-to-share-christ.html?start=1. Accessed 6 July 2018.

2   All Scripture references are in the ESV unless otherwise specified.

3   Lutes, Accessed 6 July 2018.

4   Submitted by Van Morris, *Associated Press, How Do You Spend $1.5 Billion a Year?* cbsnews.com (6-27-06) https://www.preachingtoday.com/ search/?type=&query=warren+buffet&searcharea=illustrations. Accessed 9 July 2018.

5   Chuck Herring, "How Great a Salvation" (sermon based on Ephesians 2:13 at Collierville First Baptist, preached on 1 July 2018). Accessed 9 July 2018.

6   C. H. Spurgeon, "Presumptuous Sins" (sermon based on Psalm 19:13, preached on 7 June 1857). Accessed 9 July 2018.

7   Ken Ham, "Young People Like the Bible but not Church" Ken Ham Blog. https://answersingenesis.org/blogs/ken-ham/2016/01/18/young-people-bible-not-church/. Accessed 11 July 2018.

8   Tommy Vinson, Preaching a Sermon on Salvation (First Baptist Collierville, 2014). Accessed 8 July 2018.

9   Scott Galloway, "Silicon Valleys, Tax-Avoiding, Job-Killing, Soul-Sucking Machine" Esquire. https://www.preachingtoday.com/search/ ?type=&query=google&searcharea=illustrations. Accessed 8 July 2018.

10 Chuck Herring.

11 Robby Gallaty, Discipleship Task Force Report, Southern Baptist Convention 2018. https://www.namb.net/news/disciple-making-task-force-report-bible-engagement-follow-up-to-key-discussion/. Accessed 8 July 2018.

12 Chuck Lawless, "9 Reasons Christians Don't Evangelize" http://chucklawless.com/2018/05/9-reasons-christians-dont-evangelize/. Accessed 9 July 2018.

13 Webster-Merriam, https://www.merriamwebster.com/dictionary/conversa-tionalist. Accessed 10 July 2018.

14 Cambridge Dictionary, https://dictionary.cambridge.org/dictionary/english/conversationalist. Accessed 10 July 2018.

15 Webster's II New College Dictionary (Boston, MA: Houghton Mifflin, 2005), 253.

16 English Oxford Living Dictionaries, https://en.oxforddictionaries.com/definition/conversationalist. Accessed 10 July 2018.

17 Steve Gaines, *Share Jesus Like it Matters* (Tigerville, SC: Auxano Press, 2016), 79.

18 Brian Kohout, "Stanford Admission Requirements" College Simply https://www.preachingtoday.com/illustrations/2018/july/perfection-required-for-acceptance-at-stanford-university.html. Accessed 10 July 2018.

19 Travis Bradberry and Jean Greaves *Emotional Intelligence 2.0* (San Deigo, CA: Talent Smart, 2009), 7-8.

20 Daniel Goleman, *Working With Emotional Intelligence* (New York, NY: Bantam Book, 1998), 317.

21 Roy Oswald and Arland Jacobson, *The Emotional Intelligence of Jesus: Relational Smarts for Religious Leaders* (Lanham, MD: Rowman & Littlefield), 49.

22 Daniel Goleman, "What Makes a Leader" Harvard Business Review https://hbr.org/2004/01/what-makes-a-leader. Accessed 10 July 2018.

23 Submitted by Sherman Lee Buford, *Tuskegee Institute.* https://www.preachingtoday.com/search/?query=MENSA&searcharea=illustrations&type=. Accessed 11 July 2018.

24 Submitted by Matt Svoboda Executive Pastor of Campus Development at Bridge Church in Nashville, TN. Accessed 11 July 2018.

25 Robby Gallaty, *Rediscovering Discipleship: Making Jesus' Final Words Our First Work* (Grand Rapids, MI: Zondervan, 2015), 82-84.

26 Gallaty, *Rediscovering Discipleship*, 84.

27 Gerald Stevens, "Introductory Greek Grammar" https://drkoine.com/lectures/introgk/index.html. Accessed 21 July 2018.

28 Haddon Robinson, *Biblical Preaching* (Ada, MI: Baker Academic, 2001), 100.

29 Larry Wise, *Leadership* Vol 11. No. 2. https://www.preachingtoday.com/search/?type=&query=crowds&searcharea=illustrations. Accessed 22 July 2018.

30 Logos Bible Software 4. Accessed 23 July 2018.

31 Erwin Lutzer, Pastor Emeritus of The Moody Church & Radio Pastor of Moody Church Hour. https://www.moodychurch.org. Accessed 23 July 2018.

32 Oswald and Jacobson, 73.

33 Ibid, 75.

34 Ibid, 86.

35 Ibid, 111.

36 Steve Gaines, Speaking at a Retreat in 2017.

37 Christian Smith and Melinda Lundquist Denton, "Soul Searching: The Religious and Scriptural Lives of American Teenagers" Oxford University Press. https://www.preachingtoday.com/search/?type=&query=moralistic+therapeutic+deism&searcharea=illustrations. Accessed 24 July 2018.

38 David Platt, Verge Conference. https://www.christianpost.com/news/david-platt-casual-cultural-christianity-is-leading-people-to-hell-91058/. Accessed 24 July 2018.

39 Dean Inserra, Lead Pastor at City Church Tallahassee. http://www.citychurchtallahassee.com/our-staff/. Accessed 24 July 2018.

40 Adapted from Justin Deer, "How to Share the Gospel with Cultural Christians" http://www.justindeeter.com/archives/1713. Accessed 24 July 2018.

41 W. A. Criswell, "The Hem of His Garment" https://www.wacriswell.com/sermons/1966/the-hem-of-his-garment-2/. Accessed 24 July 2018.

42 John Piper, *Desiring God* (Sisters, OR: Multnoham Publishers, 2003), 81-82.

43 Readers Digest, 6 June 1993. https://www.rd.com. Accessed 28 July 2018.

44 Chuck Herring, "Life's Greatest Question" (sermon based on Acts 16:25-31 at Collierville First Baptist, preached on 22 July 2018). Accessed 28 July 2018.

45 Anonymous quote.

46 Chuck Herring, "Fatal Attraction" (sermon based on Matthew 19:16-26 at Collierville First Baptist, preached on 26 June 2011). Accessed 29 July 2018.

47 John F. Walvoord and Roy B. Zuck, *The Bible Knowledge Commentary* Logos Bible Software 4. Accessed 31 July 2018.

Printed and bound by PG in the USA